# INTERVIEW RIGHT, HIRE RIGHT, FIRE RIGHT

### 30 Years of Honest Advice for Managers Making Decisions and Job Seekers Making Smart Choices

## MICHAEL BENDER

Interview Right, Hire Right, Fire Right

30 Years of Honest Advice for Managers Making Decisions and Job Seekers Making Smart Choices

Copyright and Legal Disclaimer

By Michael Bender

Nothing will ruin a great employee faster than watching you tolerate a bad one.

— Perry Belcher

# Contents

# Foreword

I spent 30+ years doing two things: managing people in corporate environments and navigating the minefield of diplomacy. One taught me how to build teams under pressure. The other taught me how to read people, manage egos, and make decisions when there's no perfect answer.

I'm retired now. And that changes everything about what I'm willing to say.

When you're still climbing the ladder, you filter everything. You worry about offending the wrong person, protecting relationships, maintaining your professional image. You soften your language, cite best practices instead of admitting what actually works, and hedge your bets because you might need that person's recommendation someday, or that company might hire you back as a consultant.

Those constraints don't apply to me anymore.

Most hiring and firing advice you'll find is overly sanitized. It's written by people who've never actually had to fire someone on a Monday morning and then lead a team meeting on Tuesday. It's designed to sell consulting services, not to help you actually do the job. It's full of corporate jargon, theoretical frameworks, and advice that sounds good in a seminar but falls apart the moment you're sitting across from someone whose career you're about to end.

I've been in those rooms. I've made the calls that kept people up at night. I've hired people who changed the trajectory of organizations, and I've hired people who nearly destroyed them. I've fired people I liked and kept people I didn't. I've watched good managers become tyrants and watched quiet people become leaders. I've seen what happens when you get it right, and I've lived through the consequences of getting it wrong.

My diplomatic work taught me something that applies everywhere: people are predictable. When you're negotiating between parties with conflicting interests, managing cultural differences, and trying to find common ground in high-stakes situations, you see the same patterns over and over. The person who can't take feedback in a corporate meeting behaves the same way in a diplomatic negotiation. The team member who undermines you in private will do it in public, too. The patterns don't change; only the stakes do.

I wrote this book because I don't want those lessons to disappear. Not because I think I have all the answers — I don't. But because I've learned what actually matters, and I'm tired of watching people make the same mistakes I did, just because nobody was willing to tell them the truth.

This book isn't theoretical. It's not going to teach you the "seven steps to perfect hiring" or give you a framework that works in every situation. Life doesn't work that way, and neither does managing people. What you'll get instead is what I learned the hard way: what to actually look for, what to actually watch out for, how to actually have the conversations that matter, and how to actually live with the decisions you make.

I'm direct about it because you deserve that. You're making decisions that affect people's livelihoods, your team's morale, and your organization's future. You don't need corporate speak or theoretical fluff. You need to know what works and what doesn't, based on someone who's been in the room when it mattered.

The retirement part matters too. I can tell you things I couldn't say when I was still in the game. I can admit mistakes without worrying about my reputation. I can criticize common practices without hedging. I can be honest about the complexity and the messiness of this work because I'm not trying to sell you anything or protect my career.

This is what I wish someone had told me thirty years ago. Not the polished version. The real version.

Read it. Use what works. Ignore what doesn't. But whatever you do, don't make the mistakes I did just because nobody was willing to tell you the truth.

## Introduction: Nobody Likes This Part of the Job

Let's get something straight: hiring and firing are the two most nerve-wracking things you'll ever do as a leader. I've handled both responsibilities in corner offices and cramped foreign consulates, across three continents and more time zones than I can remember. I wasn't born with a magic wand. I've made mistakes, learned the hard way, and — with any luck — come out a little wiser and a lot less sentimental.

Nobody tells you this: every hiring decision you make ripples through your organization for months or years. Hire the wrong person, and you don't just waste salary and benefits. You demoralize your best people who have to pick up the slack. You lose clients who get subpar service. You spend hours in damage control meetings instead of doing actual work. A single bad hire cost a company I worked with six figures in lost productivity, not counting the recruit-ment costs to replace them.

And firing? That's even higher stakes. Fire someone poorly, and you risk lawsuits, sure. But you also risk destroying team morale, losing institutional knowledge, and creating a culture of fear where people spend more time covering their asses than doing their jobs. Fire someone too late, and you've already lost your best performers who got tired of carrying dead weight. Fire someone too early, and you look impulsive and erratic. There's no margin for error, and yet most leaders get almost no real training on how to do it right.

The conventional wisdom is worse than useless — it's actively harmful. I've sat through countless HR seminars where they tell you to "hire for culture fit" without defining what that actually means.

I've watched leaders follow the advice to "give everyone a chance" until their entire team quit in frustration. I've seen companies use the same interview questions for every role because some consultant told them it creates "consistency," even though asking a software engineer and a salesperson the same questions is idiotic.

Take this example: A CEO I worked with religiously followed the advice to "hire slow, fire fast." Sounds smart, right? Except he was so slow and deliberate about hiring that his team was chronically understaffed, burning out his best people while he waited for the "perfect" candidate who didn't exist. Meanwhile, when someone underperformed, he'd panic and fire them within weeks, without any real documentation or performance improvement plan. His team had zero trust in his judgment. The advice wasn't wrong in theory — it was just useless without context. I'll come back to what this advice actually means when you're not using it as a cop-out — but for now, know that catchy phrases don't replace judgment.

Or take the classic "hire for attitude, train for skill." Early in my career, I followed that advice and hired an enthusiastic, positive guy who couldn't actually do the technical work the role required. Six months later, after thousands of dollars in training and countless hours of my time coaching him, he still couldn't perform. Meanwhile, I'd passed on a candidate who was technically brilliant but seemed "too serious" in the interview. That serious candidate went to a competitor and became their top performer. Lesson learned: attitude matters, but competence matters more.

This book is not legal advice. I'm not your lawyer. This is the stuff you learn when you're the person everyone expects to solve people's problems, whether those people are software engineers, junior diplomats, or the guy who just can't stop showing up late.

What you'll find in these pages is a roadmap for the decisions nobody prepares you for. We'll start by dismantling the hiring myths that waste your time and money. Then we'll talk about building actual teams — not the fake "we're a family" nonsense that makes firing impossible. You'll learn how to spot the difference between someone who interviews well and someone who actually delivers, and how to recognize red flags before they become disasters. We'll cover onboarding that actually sets people up to succeed, managing underperformance without being a pushover, and firing people in a way that's honest and humane, not cruel.

This book is for anyone who has to make people decisions: new managers who are terrified of screwing up, experienced leaders who know they need to get better at this, and everyone in between who's tired of advice that sounds good in a conference room but falls apart in real life. If you're in HR, you'll probably disagree with some of what I say. If you're a leader who's lost sleep over a hiring or firing decision, you'll recognize yourself in these pages.

It's just the truth, as I've lived it: what works, what doesn't, and the stuff nobody tells you until you're sitting across from someone whose world you're about to change, for better or worse.

So, if you want platitudes and pep talks, close this book. If you want to actually get the job done — and sleep at night — keep reading.

### Who This Book Is For

This book has two audiences. Both matter equally.

### If you're a manager or leader:

You're here because you're tired of hiring advice that doesn't work in the real world. Maybe you're a new manager terrified of your first hire or your first firing. Maybe you're experienced but you know you're not as good at this as you should be. Maybe you're an HR professional drowning in theory that doesn't translate to actual people. Maybe you're a small business owner doing all of this your-self with no safety net. Or maybe you've just lost sleep over a people decision and you want to stop doing that.

This book is for you. It's not going to tell you to hire for "culture fit" or fire people with a smile. It's going to tell you what actually works, what doesn't, and how to make decisions you can live with.

### If you're a job seeker or employee:

You're here because you want to understand what's actually happening on the other side of the table. You're interviewing and you want to know what managers are really looking for — not what they say they're looking for. You're wondering if you should stay at your current job or get out. You've been burned by a bad company and you don't want it to happen again. You're negotiating salary and you want to know if you're being played. You're changing careers and you're not sure how to position yourself.

This book is for you too. You'll learn how to spot a good manager before you work for them, how to protect yourself in negotiations, and how to recognize when it's time to walk.

**The point:** This isn't a management book that ignores job seekers, or a career book that ignores what managers actually think. It's both. Because better hiring and firing decisions happen when both sides understand what's really going on.

Read the parts that apply to you. But read the other side too. You'll make better decisions when you understand how the other person thinks.

# Why Most Hiring Advice Misses the Mark

Let's cut through the noise. The internet is full of hiring "secrets" that don't survive contact with real life. Culture fit? Overrated. Gut instinct? Sometimes it's just indigestion. Fancy questions about spirit animals or "synergy"? Please.

I've sat through hiring workshops where consultants with zero real-world management experience told me to "hire for attitude, train for skill" and "look for passion." That's great until you hire someone passionate about all the wrong things, or someone with a fantastic attitude who can't actually do the job you're paying them for.

The worst advice I ever followed came from a leadership guru who said, "If you're not 100% excited about a candidate, pass." Sounds good, right? Except I passed on three strong candidates because they didn't give me goosebumps, and then spent six months understaffed while my team burned out. Meanwhile, the "exciting" candidate I eventually hired turned out to be a nightmare who talked a great game but delivered nothing.

What actually matters when you're hiring:

**1. Can they actually do the job?**

Not "do they have the right degree" or "did they work at a fancy company." Can they execute the specific tasks you need done, at the level you need them done? Everything else is window dressing.

A guy with an MBA from a top-ten school taught me this lesson the hard way. On paper, he was perfect for a project management role. In reality, he couldn't organize a two-car parade. He'd never actually run a project from start to finish — he'd been the "strategic advisor" who swooped in for meetings and left the real work to others.

Meanwhile, the best project manager I ever hired had a community college degree and had worked her way up from an administrative assistant. She knew how to build timelines, manage stakeholders, and actually get things across the finish line because she'd done it a hundred times.

Test for this: Don't just ask about their experience. Give them a real scenario from your workplace and ask them to walk you through how they'd handle it. Listen for specifics. If they're vague or theoretical, they're guessing. If they give you a step-by-step breakdown with potential pitfalls identified, they know what they're doing.

**2. Do they finish what they start?**

Look at their track record. Not their resume — their actual history of completion. People who leave a trail of half-finished projects will do the same for you.

This is where reference checks actually matter. Don't just call the references they give you (those are always going to be friendly). Do some digging. Find people they worked with who aren't on their list. Ask specific questions: "Tell me about a project they led from beginning to end. What was the outcome? Did they hit their deadlines?"

One hire had worked at four companies in three years. Each time, he'd "led major initiatives" that sounded impressive. When I dug deeper after he flamed out with us, I found out that every single one of those initiatives had been abandoned or handed off to someone else to finish. He was great at starting things and terrible at the hard middle part, where you actually have to deliver.

Red flag: If someone's resume is full of "launched," "initiated," and "spearheaded" but light on "completed," "delivered," and "achieved," you're looking at a starter, not a finisher.

### 3. Will they tell you the truth when it's uncomfortable?

You don't need yes-men. You need people who'll tell you when something's broken, when a deadline's impossible, or when your idea needs work. Test for this in the interview. Push back on something they say and see if they fold or stand their ground.

A script I've used: When a candidate tells me about a success, I'll say something like, "That's interesting, but I'm not sure I agree with your approach. I think [alternative approach] would have been better." Then I shut up and watch.

The yes-men immediately backpedal: "Oh, you're right, we should have done it that way." The good ones push back: "I can see why you'd think that, but here's why we chose our approach..." and then they defend their reasoning with facts.

A candidate once told me flat-out in the interview that one of my questions was based on a flawed assumption. She was polite but firm. I was impressed. She turned out to be one of the best hires I ever made because she wasn't afraid to tell me when I was wrong — and she was usually right.

### 4. Can they handle ambiguity without melting down?

Most jobs aren't paint-by-numbers. Things change. Priorities shift. Resources disappear. You need people who can navigate fog without needing their hand held every five minutes.

The best way to test this is to give them an ambiguous problem during the interview. Something like, "We need to enter a new market, but we're not sure which one. We have a limited budget and six months. How would you approach this?"

Listen to how they handle the uncertainty. Do they immediately ask for more information (good)? Do they freeze up (bad)? Do they start making assumptions and building a framework (very good)?

Two candidates for the same role got the same ambiguous scenario. The first one said, "I'd need more data before I could answer that." The second one said, "First, I'd identify our top three criteria for market selection. Then I'd do rapid research on five potential markets using these free resources. Within two weeks, I'd have a recommendation with a risk assessment for each option."

Guess who got the job?

The people who thrive in ambiguity are the ones who can build structure where none exists. They don't wait for perfect information — they make reasonable assumptions, test them quickly, and adjust as they learn.

## 5. Do they make the people around them better or worse?

One toxic hire can crater a whole team. One great hire can lift everyone's game. Pay attention to how they talk about past colleagues, past bosses, past projects. If everyone else was always the problem, guess who the problem actually was.

Listen to the language they use. Do they say "I" or "we"? Do they give credit to others or take it all for themselves? When they talk about conflicts, do they show any self-awareness about their own role?

A candidate spent 20 minutes telling me about all the incompetent people he'd worked with. His boss was clueless. His colleagues were lazy. His direct reports were idiots. Every story was about how he was the only competent person in the room.

I didn't hire him. Six months later, I ran into someone who'd worked with him. She told me he'd been fired for creating a toxic environment that led three people to quit in one month.

Contrast that with a candidate who told me about a project that failed. She said, "I pushed too hard for my approach and didn't listen to the concerns my team was raising. By the time I realized they were right, we'd wasted two months going down the wrong path. I learned to slow down and really hear what people are telling me."

That's self-awareness. That's someone who makes those around them better by being willing to learn and adapt.

### The Five-Question Framework in Action

I kept a scorecard. For each candidate, I rate them on each question: Strong, Adequate, or Weak. If they're weak on more than one, they're out. If they're strong on at least three and adequate on the others, they move forward.

This isn't scientific. It's not perfect. But it's kept me from making most of the hiring mistakes I used to make when I went on gut feel or got dazzled by credentials.

**What This Means for Your Hiring Process**

Stop asking ineffective interview questions. "Where do you see yourself in five years?" tells you nothing. "Tell me about a time you demonstrated leadership" gets you rehearsed stories.

Instead, ask:

• "Walk me through a project you completed from start to finish. What obstacles did you hit and how did you handle them?" (Tests for completion and problem-solving)

• "Tell me about a time you disagreed with your boss. What happened?" (Tests for truth-telling)

• "Here's a real problem we're facing right now. How would you approach it?" (Tests for handling ambiguity)

• "Tell me about the best team you've ever been on. What made it great? What was your role in that?" (Tests for team impact)

And nobody tells you this: You're going to get it wrong sometimes anyway. Even with a great process, you'll hire people who don't work out. The goal isn't perfection — it's improving your odds and failing faster when you do get it wrong.

That's it. Five things. Not fifty. Not some elaborate personality matrix or four-hour assessment center. Just five questions that, if you answer them honestly, will save you from 90% of hiring disasters.

The rest of this book is about how to actually figure out these answers — and what to do when you get them wrong.

# 2

# Building a Real
# Team (Not a Family)

Let's address the most problematic myth in business: "We're a family here." No, you're not. You're a unit on a mission, and your mission isn't unconditional love — it's results. Families put up with Uncle Larry even when he ruins Thanksgiving. Teams bench or cut the weak link, or they lose.

A company I worked at had a CEO who loved to talk about how "we're all family here." He meant well. But what it actually created was a culture where nobody could be held accountable because "we don't give up on family." Underperformers stuck around for years. Toxic behavior got excused. And the high performers? They left because they were tired of carrying dead weight.

The family metaphor sounds warm and fuzzy, but it's a trap. It confuses professional relationships with personal ones. It makes people feel guilty for setting boundaries or making tough calls. And it sets up unrealistic expectations on both sides.

The truth: You're not building a family. You're building a team. And teams have a different set of rules.

### The Difference Between Teams and Families

Families are permanent. Teams are conditional. You're on the team as long as you contribute to the mission. That's not cruel — it's honest.

Families forgive everything. Teams forgive mistakes but not patterns. One screw-up? We'll work through it. Repeated failures? You're out.

Families prioritize feelings. Teams prioritize results. That doesn't mean you're heartless — it means you're clear about what matters.

The military taught me this distinction, where team cohesion is literally life-or-death. You trust your team with everything, but if someone can't do their job, they get reassigned. It's not personal. It's survival.

## How to Actually Build a Team
### Set the Standard Early

Day one, let people know what "good" looks like. Not just the job description — the attitude, the pace, the level of honesty you expect.

I start every new hire's first day with a conversation that goes something like this: "Here's what success looks like in this role. Here's what will get you promoted. And here's what will get you fired. I'm not going to sugarcoat things or wait until your 90-day review to tell you if something's wrong. If I have feedback, you'll hear it right away. And I expect the same from you."

Some people find this jarring. They're used to the corporate dance where nobody says what they really mean. But the ones who thrive appreciate the clarity. They know exactly where they stand.

I also share examples of what good work looks like. Not just abstract standards, but actual work product from high performers (with permission, obviously). "This is what a great project plan looks like. This is what a solid client presentation looks like. This is the bar."

### No Sacred Cows

Nobody is untouchable. Not your best salesperson, not your oldest friend from college. The minute people think someone is above the rules, you lose the team.

A team I managed had a top salesperson who was a complete jerk. He hit his numbers, so leadership let him get away with murder. He'd yell at support staff, miss meetings, and ignore processes. Everyone hated him, but nobody would touch him because of his sales numbers.

Then one quarter, his numbers slipped. And suddenly, all the behavior that had been "tolerated" became a problem. He got fired, and the team's reaction told me everything: They were relieved, not upset. Morale actually went up, even though we'd lost our top producer.

What I learned: That guy's numbers were good, but they weren't as good as they looked. He was hoarding leads, taking credit for team efforts, and his behavior was driving away support staff who could have helped everyone sell more. When we replaced him with someone who was 80% as good but 1000% better to work with, overall team performance went up.

The rule is simple: High performance doesn't buy you permission to be toxic. If you can't follow the basic rules of professional behavior, you're out, no matter what your numbers are.

## Encourage Healthy Conflict

Teams that never argue aren't teams — they're scared. You want people to challenge each other, to push for better. Your job is to keep it respectful and productive.

The best teams I've led had vigorous debates. People disagreed openly, defended their positions with data, and sometimes got heated. But it was always about the work, never personal.

Creating that culture requires three things:

First, model it yourself. When someone challenges your idea, don't get defensive. Say, "That's a good point. Tell me more about why you think that." Show that disagreement is safe.

Second, set ground rules. Debate the idea, not the person. Bring data, not just opinions. And once a decision is made, everyone commits — even if they disagreed.

Third, shut down personal attacks immediately. The moment someone makes it about the person instead of the idea, you step in: "Hold on. Let's keep this about the work."

Two team members disagreed about everything. Every meeting turned into a debate between them. Some managers would have seen this as a problem. I saw it as an asset, because they were both smart and they pushed each other to sharpen their thinking. The key was making sure it stayed productive.

One day, one of them crossed the line and made a personal comment. I pulled them both aside after the meeting and said, "You two challenging each other makes us better. But the personal stuff stops now. Debate the work, respect the person." They got it. The debates continued, but the personal jabs stopped.

### Reward Team Players, Not Lone Wolves

Celebrate the folks who lift others up. Lone geniuses are great... until they're not. If someone can't pass the ball, they don't belong on the court.

I used to think the highest performers were the ones who produced the most individually. Then I started tracking team performance more carefully and realized something: The people who made everyone around them better were more valuable than the individual superstars.

A team member was good at her job — not the best, but solid. But she had this habit of helping everyone else get better. She'd mentor new hires, share her shortcuts and templates, and jump in to help when someone was stuck. Her individual numbers were middle of the pack, but the team's overall performance was 20% higher when she was there than when she was out.

I started recognizing this explicitly. In team meetings, I'd call out not just who hit their numbers, but who helped others hit theirs. I adjusted our bonus structure to include a team component, not just individual performance. And I made it clear in hiring and promotions that being a team player wasn't optional — it was part of the job.

The lone wolves hated this. A couple of them left. And you know what? We were better off without them.

### Make the Mission Bigger Than Any One Person

If you build a culture where the mission matters more than egos, people will step up — and step aside — for the good of the team.

This is where leadership actually matters. You have to articulate a mission that people care about. Not some corporate nonsense about "maximizing shareholder value," but something real.

When I led a team in a diplomatic post, the mission was clear: Keep people safe and help them navigate a complex foreign system. Everyone on the team understood that when things got tough, the mission came first. Personal preferences, career advancement, office politics — all of that was secondary.

In the private sector, it's harder because the mission is often less clear. But you can still create it. Maybe it's "Build products that actually solve customer problems." Maybe it's "Be the team that other teams can count on." Maybe it's "Do work we're proud of."

Whatever it is, you have to mean it. And you have to make decisions that reinforce it, even when it's costly.

My best performer had to be pulled off a high-profile project because the project needed someone with a different skill set. He was upset. But I explained: "The mission is to deliver this project successfully. You're great, but you're not the right fit for this particular challenge. I need you on something else where you can have more impact."

He didn't like it, but he respected it. Because he knew I was making the call based on the mission, not politics or favoritism.

**What This Actually Looks Like Day-to-Day**

Building a real team isn't about trust falls and team-building exercises (though if those work for you, fine). It's about:

• Giving people direct feedback in the moment, not waiting for reviews
• Celebrating team wins, not just individual ones
• Making tough calls about who stays and who goes based on contribution, not tenure
• Being honest about what's working and what's not
• Trusting people to do their jobs without micromanaging
• Holding everyone to the same standards, including yourself

**The Test of a Real Team**

You know if you've built a real team by what happens when someone leaves (voluntarily or not). Does the team rally and step up, or does it fall apart?

Real teams have resilience. They're not dependent on any one person, including you. They have shared standards, mutual accountability, and a mission they believe in.

Fake teams (or "families") fall apart the minute there's conflict or change. Because they were never really a team — they were just a group of people who happened to work together.

You don't need a family. You need a squad you trust to get the job done. Treat them like professionals, not relatives, and watch what happens.

# 3

# How to Spot Winners – and Weed Out Fakers

The world is full of people who look great on paper and sound great in interviews — but turn into dead weight the minute you need them. Winners aren't always the loudest, the flashiest, or the ones with the most certificates on the wall.

I've been fooled by smooth talkers more times than I'd like to admit. The candidate who had an answer for everything, who made me laugh, who seemed like they'd fit right in. Then they started, and it turned out all that charm was covering up a complete lack of substance.

And I've almost passed on quiet, unassuming candidates who turned out to be absolute rockstars. The ones who didn't sell themselves well in interviews but delivered consistently once they were on the job.

Over time, I've learned to look past the performance and focus on the evidence. What actually separates winners from fakers:

**Spotting the Real Deal**

**Ask About Failure, Not Success**

Anyone can rattle off their wins. Ask about their biggest screw-up. Did they own it or blame everyone else? Winners learn from pain. Fakers dodge or spin.

My go-to question: "Tell me about a time you really screwed something up. What happened, what was your role in it, and what did you learn?"

The fakers will either claim they've never really failed (red flag), or they'll tell you a story where they were the victim of circumstances beyond their control. "My boss didn't give me the resources I needed." "The client changed their mind at the last minute." "My team didn't execute."

Notice the pattern? It's never their fault.

Winners tell you a different story. They'll say something like: "I pushed a product launch without doing enough user testing because I was overconfident. It flopped. We had to pull it back, fix it, and relaunch three months later. I learned that my gut isn't always right and that I need to validate assumptions before betting big."

That's ownership. That's self-awareness. That's someone who learns.

One hire told me about a project where he'd been so focused on hitting a deadline that he ignored quality concerns his team was raising. They shipped on time, but the product was buggy, and customers were furious. He said, "I was so worried about looking bad for missing the deadline that I made us look worse by shipping a flawed product. Now I know that a delayed launch is better than a broken product."

He turned out to be one of the most reliable people I've ever worked with, because he'd learned that lesson the hard way and never forgot it.

### Pressure Test

Give them a real problem to solve — something messy, with no perfect answer. Winners wade in. Fakers flounder or freeze.

I kept a few real scenarios from my workplace in my back pocket for interviews. Not hypotheticals, but actual problems we've faced. I'll say, "Here's a situation we dealt with last quarter. How would you approach it?"

Then I watched what they did.

The fakers will either give you a textbook answer that sounds good but isn't practical, or they'll ask a million clarifying questions to avoid actually answering. They're stalling because they don't know what to do.

The winners will think for a moment, then start working through it out loud. "Okay, first I'd want to understand X. Assuming that's the case, I'd probably do Y, but if it turns out to be Z, I'd pivot to this other approach. The biggest risk I see is..."

They're not trying to give you the "right" answer. They're showing you how they think.

A candidate got a scenario about a project that was over budget and behind schedule, with an impatient client. She said, "First, I'd get everyone in a room — the team, the client, and any key stakeholders. I'd put all the cards on the table: here's where we are, here's why, here's what it'll take to finish. Then I'd give the client options: we can cut scope and deliver on time, or we can deliver everything, but it'll take longer and cost more. But I wouldn't let it drag on with everyone pretending things are fine when they're not."

That's a winner. She didn't have a magic solution, but she had a clear process for dealing with a messy situation.

### Watch How They Treat People Who Can't Help Them

Receptionists, interns, waitstaff. Winners are decent across the board. Fakers save their charm for the boss.

A mentor taught me this trick — he always took candidates to lunch and watched how they treated the server. If they were rude or dismissive, the interview was over, no matter how impressive they were otherwise.

I did something similar. I have my assistant or a junior team member greet candidates upon arrival. Later, I'll ask, "How did they treat you?" If the answer is anything other than "They were friendly and respectful," that's a red flag.

A candidate who was charming and impressive in the interview had been condescending to my assistant when she offered him coffee, as if she were beneath him. I didn't hire him.

Six months later, I heard from someone at his new company that he was a nightmare to work with — great with executives, terrible with everyone else.

How people treat those who can't help them tells you who they really are.

### Check Their Curiosity Level

Winners are always learning. If they haven't read a book, taken a course, or learned a new skill in the past year, beware.

I ask candidates: "What have you learned recently? What are you working on getting better at?"

Fakers will either draw a blank or give you something vague like "I'm always learning on the job." Winners will light up and tell you about a specific skill they're developing, a book that changed their thinking, or a course they're taking.

One hire told me she'd been teaching herself data analysis because she realized she was making too many decisions based on gut feel. She'd taken an online course, was working through practice problems, and had started applying it to her current job. That's someone who's going to keep growing.

Contrast that with a candidate who told me he didn't really have time for learning outside of work. He'd been doing the same job the same way for five years. That's someone who's going to stagnate.

### Gut Check Isn't Enough

Your gut can be fooled by charisma, looks, or shared interests. Back it up with evidence. Call old bosses. Give practical tests.

I used to trust my gut a lot. If I "clicked" with someone in an interview, I'd hire them. If something felt off, I'd pass.

Then I started tracking my gut-based decisions and realized I was wrong about 40% of the time. That's a terrible batting average.

Then I used my gut as one data point, but I backed it up with evidence:

- Reference checks (real ones, not just the names they give you)
- Work samples or practical tests
- Multiple interviews with different people on the team
- Structured questions that everyone gets asked

My gut still matters — if something feels really off, I pay attention. But I don't let it override evidence.

### Weeding Out the Fakers
### Never Rush

Desperation hires are almost always disasters. Hold out for the right fit.

I know the pressure. You're understaffed, your team is burning out, and you need someone yesterday. But hiring the wrong person makes everything worse.

Hiring someone in a panic because we were drowning taught me this lesson. She was available immediately and seemed okay in the interview — not great, but good enough. Within two months, I realized she couldn't do the job. I spent the next four months managing her out while also doing her work. If I'd just held out for another month and found the right person, I would have saved myself six months of misery.

The rule: It's better to be understaffed with good people than fully staffed with dead weight.

**Don't Fall for Drama**

If someone's story is "everyone else is an idiot," believe them — and run.

Some candidates are really good at making themselves sound like the hero of every story. They were the only competent person at their last company. Their boss was incompetent. Their colleagues were lazy. They single-handedly saved every project.

This is a massive red flag. Because either they're lying, or they're impossible to work with, or both.

A candidate I met spent the entire time telling me how much smarter he was than everyone at his previous companies. He'd worked at three well-respected firms, and according to him, they were all full of idiots.

I didn't hire him. Later, I talked to someone who'd worked with him. She said, "He's smart, but he's so arrogant that nobody wants to work with him. He alienates everyone and then wonders why his projects fail."

Winners give credit to others. They talk about what they learned from colleagues and bosses. They acknowledge that success is a team effort. If someone can't do that, they're not a winner — they're a faker with an ego problem.

**Probe for Accountability**

Winners say, "Here's where I screwed up, here's what I learned." Fakers say, "That wasn't my fault."

This comes back to the failure question, but it's worth emphasizing. The single best predictor of success is taking responsibility for mistakes.

I ask follow-up questions when candidates tell me about failures: "What would you do differently if you could do it over?" "What was your role in what went wrong?" "How did you make sure you didn't make that mistake again?"

Winners have clear, specific answers. Fakers get vague or defensive.

### The Winner's Profile

After years of hiring, what winners have in common:
- They own their mistakes and learn from them
- They're curious and always developing new skills
- They treat everyone with respect, regardless of status
- They can handle ambiguity and complexity
- They give credit to others and take responsibility themselves
- They have a track record of finishing what they start
- They're honest, even when it's uncomfortable

If you find someone with most of these traits, hire them. Even if they're not perfect on paper. Even if they're not the most charismatic person in the room.

Because winners deliver. And in the long run, that's all that matters.

What you do: Print that list above. Keep it in front of you during every interview. Ask questions that reveal these traits, then actually listen to the answers. Because every faker you hire costs you three good people who get tired of carrying them.

4

# The Money Talk: How to Discuss Salary Without Getting Screwed (Either Side)

Nobody wants to talk about money, and that's exactly why everyone messes it up.

I've watched hiring managers dance around salary like it's a state secret. I've watched candidates play coy about their expectations like they're negotiating a hostage release. And I've been on both sides myself — badly — until I learned that all this game-playing is counterproductive.

The truth: if you can't be straight about money, you can't be straight about anything. And if you start a working relationship with games and dishonesty, that's the foundation you're building on.

This chapter is for both sides because I've been on both sides. I've hired hundreds of people. I've been hired. I've negotiated from positions of strength and desperation. And I've learned that transparency beats tactics every single time.

For Hiring Managers: Stop Playing Games

Bring Up Money Early

The biggest mistake I saw managers make is waiting until the end of the interview process to discuss salary. You spend weeks interviewing someone, everyone falls in love with them, and then you find out they want $40K more than you can pay.

That's not a negotiation. That's a waste of everyone's time.

I learned to raise salary in the first conversation — not the exact number, but the range. "Before we go further, I want to make sure we're in the same ballpark. This role has a budget of $X to $Y. Does that work for you?"

If they say no, you've saved yourself weeks of pointless interviews. If they say yes, you can focus on whether they're the right person, not whether you can afford them.

Be Honest About Your Budget

Early in my career, I tried to lowball a candidate because I thought I could hire her for less than her asking price. She was early in her career, and I figured she didn't know her market value.

She took the offer. And six months later, she found out what her peers were making and felt cheated. She left for a competitor who paid her fairly, and I had to start the hiring process over.

I didn't save money. I lost a good employee and spent more recruiting and training her replacement.

What I should have done: paid her what she was worth from the start. If I couldn't afford her, I should have said so and moved on.

When They're Outside Your Range

Sometimes you meet someone perfect who costs more than you budgeted. You have three options:

1. Find the money. Go back to your budget. Can you move things around? Can you make the case for a higher salary? If this person is truly exceptional, it might be worth it.

2. Offer non-salary compensation. Equity, flexibility, faster promotion track, professional development budget. Some people value these as much as cash. But don't mislead them — if you're offering "growth opportunities" instead of money, be specific about what that means.

3. Let them go. If you can't afford them and can't offer something else of value, be honest: "You're great, but you're outside our budget and I can't close that gap. I don't want to waste your time."

What you don't do is string them along hoping they'll magically lower their expectations.

The Script That Works

"I want to be transparent about compensation. The range for this role is $X to $Y, depending on experience. Based on what I've seen so far, I'd likely come in around $Z. Does that work for you, or are we too far apart?"

Then shut up and listen.

If they counter, you negotiate like adults. If they say it's too low, you either find more money or you part ways. But at least you're both dealing with reality.

For Job Seekers: Know Your Worth and Ask for It

Do Your Homework

Before you walk into any salary discussion, know what you're worth. Not what you want. Not what you made at your last job. What the market pays for your skills and experience.

I've seen people undersell themselves by $20K because they didn't research. I've also seen people price themselves out of jobs because they overestimated their value.

Use Glassdoor, Payscale, industry surveys, and your network. Talk to recruiters. Get multiple data points. Then add context: your location, your specific skills, the company size, the industry.

The "Current Salary" Trap

There's a question I don't like: "What's your current salary?"

It's a trap. If you're underpaid now, you'll be underpaid in the new job. If you're overpaid, they'll lowball you.

Some states have banned this question, but plenty of interviewers still ask it. Here's how I learned to handle it:

"I'd prefer to focus on the value I'd bring to this role rather than what I'm currently making. Based on my research, the market rate for this position is $X to $Y. Is that in line with your budget?"

If they push, you can say: "My current compensation is part of a total package that's hard to compare directly. I'm looking for $X in this role based on the responsibilities and market rates."

You're not lying. You're redirecting to what matters: what this job should pay, not what your last job did pay.

How to State Your Expectations

One of my hires handled this perfectly. I asked about his salary expectations, and he said:

"Based on my research and the scope of this role, I'm looking for something in the $X to $Y range. I'm flexible depending on the total package, but that's the ballpark I'm targeting. Does that work with your budget?"

Clear. Confident. Not apologetic. Not aggressive. Just stating a fact.

I respected that. We were within range, so we kept talking. If we hadn't been, we would have saved each other time.

### When to Walk Away

I've walked away from job offers over money twice in my career. Both times, it was the right call.

The first time, the company kept lowballing me and acting like I should be grateful for the opportunity. The salary was 20% below market, and when I pointed that out, they got defensive. That told me everything I needed to know about how they valued people.

The second time, the salary was fine, but they kept changing the terms. First it was $X, then it was $X minus 10% with a "performance bonus" that was entirely discretionary. That's not negotiation. That's bait-and-switch.

If a company won't pay you fairly, or if they play games during the offer stage, it won't get better after you're hired. Walk away.

### Why Underselling Yourself Hurts Long-Term

Let's say you take a job for $10K less than you're worth because you really want the role. You think you'll prove yourself and get a raise later.

What actually happens: your salary becomes your baseline. Your raises are percentages of that baseline. You're now permanently behind where you should be.

And when you go to your next job, they'll ask what you're currently making, and you're starting from a lower number again.

I've seen people lose hundreds of thousands of dollars over their careers because they undervalued themselves once and never caught up.

Don't do that. Ask for what you're worth. If they can't pay it, that's fine — but don't negotiate against yourself.

### What Both Sides Get Wrong

Stop Playing Chicken

The least productive thing both sides do is wait for the other person to name a number first. The hiring manager won't share the budget. The candidate won't share their expectations. Everyone's trying to gain leverage, and all it does is waste time.

Just put the numbers on the table. You're both adults. You both know this is a business transaction. Stop pretending it's something else.

"Fair Compensation" is Subjective

Nobody wants to admit this: there's no objective "fair" salary. There's market rate, there's what the company can afford, and there's what the candidate will accept. Those three things don't always align.

A startup might not be able to match a corporate salary, but they can offer equity and faster growth. A corporate job might pay more but offer less flexibility. A nonprofit might pay less but offer more meaningful work.

"Fair" depends on what you value. Be honest about that.

Non-Salary Compensation That Actually Matters

I've seen candidates turn down higher salaries for:
• Real equity (not token options that'll never vest)
• Remote work or flexible hours
• Better health insurance or retirement matching
• Professional development budgets
• Faster path to leadership

And I've seen hiring managers close deals by offering these things when they couldn't offer more cash.

But it has to be real. Don't promise "unlimited growth potential" when you mean "we'll work you to death for the same salary." Don't offer "equity" that's worthless. Be specific about what you're offering and why it has value.

When Money Isn't the Real Issue

Sometimes salary negotiations break down, and it's not really about the money.

I've had candidates who kept pushing for more because they

didn't trust the company. I've had hiring managers who wouldn't budge because they didn't think the candidate was committed.

If you're stuck on salary, ask yourself: is this really about the number, or is it about something else? Respect? Trust? Fear of being taken advantage of?

If it's not really about money, more money won't fix it.

Red Flags in Salary Discussions

From the Employer:

• Won't share a salary range even when directly asked

• Keeps moving the goalposts ("Actually, the budget is lower than I thought")

• Pressures you to decide immediately

• Makes you feel greedy for negotiating

• Promises big raises "once you prove yourself," but won't put anything in writing

From the Candidate:

• Won't give any indication of their expectations

• Demands way above market rate with no justification

• Keeps bringing up salary in every conversation before there's an offer

• Uses other offers as leverage in a manipulative way (vs. transparently)

• Acts are entitled to a certain salary without demonstrating the value

Difficult Scenarios I've Navigated

The Candidate You Love Who's Out of Budget

I found a perfect candidate once who wanted $30K more than I'd budgeted. I went back to my boss and made the case: "This person will do the work of two people. We can pay her $X and get exceptional results, or pay someone $Y and get mediocre results. Which is cheaper?"

We found the money. She was worth every penny.

But I've also had times when I couldn't find the money, and I had to let great people go. It's difficult, but it's reality.

Internal Equity Issues

This is the nightmare scenario: you need to hire someone at a salary that's higher than your existing team members make.

I've been there. You have two choices. Either you bring your existing team up (which is expensive but fair), or you don't make the hire.

What you don't do is hire someone at a higher salary and hope your team doesn't find out. They will find out. And when they do, you'll lose their trust and probably lose them.

Counteroffers

When you're hiring someone and their current employer makes a counteroffer, you're usually in a tough spot. If they accept the counteroffer, you've wasted time. If they turn it down and come to you, you're always wondering if they're just using you as leverage for the next raise.

I learned to ask candidates early: "If your current employer counters, what would you do?" If they hesitate or say "it depends," they're not really ready to leave.

The Bottom Line

Salary discussions tell you everything you need to know. Can you be direct? Can you handle conflict? Can you respect someone enough to tell them the truth?

If you can't talk about money like adults, you won't work together like adults.

What to do right now:

**If you're hiring:** Know your budget before you post the job. Don't waste anyone's time — including yours.

# 5

# For the Job Seeker: How to Protect Yourself and Pick the Right Place

I've spent most of this book talking to employers. But I've also been the candidate. I've taken jobs I shouldn't have, ignored red flags, and stayed too long at places that were killing my career. So let me flip the script and tell you what I wish someone had told me.

### Do Your Homework Before You Walk In

A candidate once showed up to an interview and asked me what our company did. Not in a curious way — in a "I have no idea" way. I explained our business model, our market position, our revenue streams. He nodded along, asked a few generic questions, and left. I never called him back.

Here's what I learned: if you don't care enough to spend 20 minutes learning about a company before you interview there, why should they care about hiring you? It's not about being perfect. It's about showing respect for their time and yours.

Before you walk into any interview, you need to know three things: what the company does, who you're talking to, and what's actually happening there right now.

Start with the basics. Go to their website. Read their "About Us" page. Look at their product or service. Understand their business model. If you can't explain what they do in one sentence after 10 minutes of research, that's a red flag about the company, not you. Some companies are deliberately vague because they don't know what they're doing either.

Then dig into recent news. Google the company name. Check their LinkedIn page. Look for press releases, funding announcements, or recent hires. If they just laid off 20% of their staff, you need to know that before you walk in. If they just landed a huge client, that's worth mentioning. This isn't about being a stalker — it's about being informed.

Finally, find out who you're actually talking to. Look them up on LinkedIn. See what their background is. What's their title? How long have they been there? What did they do before? This gives you context for the conversation and helps you ask smarter questions. It also shows them you did your homework.

**Your Resume and Application: What Actually Matters**

Here's the truth about resumes: I spend about 30 seconds on each one. That's it. In those 30 seconds, I'm looking for one thing: does this person have the experience we need, and can they communicate it clearly?

Most resumes fail that test immediately. Not because the person isn't qualified, but because they don't know how to present themselves.

When I'm scanning a resume, here's what actually gets my attention: specific achievements with numbers attached to them. Not "responsible for sales growth" — that tells me nothing. But "grew territory revenue from $2M to $5.2M in 18 months" or "reduced customer churn by 23% through implementation of new retention program" — that's real. That's something I can picture. That's something I can ask about in an interview.

I also want to see clear progression. Did you move up? Did you take on bigger responsibilities? Did you move between companies strategically, or are you just job-hopping? Your resume should tell a story about where you've been and where you're going. If I can't see that story in 30 seconds, I'm moving on.

What gets ignored: objective statements. "Seeking a challenging position where I can utilize my skills and grow professionally." That's meaningless. Every candidate says that. Skip it. I also ignore skill lists that have no context. "Microsoft Excel, Salesforce, project management, communication" — okay, but what did you actually do with those skills? Show me, don't tell me.

Huge walls of text are a no. If I have to squint to read your resume, I'm not going to. Use white space. Use bullet points. Make it scannable. And for God's sake, no obvious lies. I've seen people claim they managed teams they didn't manage, led projects they just participated in, or had titles they never actually held. I always check references, and when the story doesn't match, that person is done. It's not worth the risk.

One of my best hires had been a barista, then a junior accountant, then a marketing coordinator, then a sales rep. On paper, it looked scattered. But the cover letter explained it: she was building skills intentionally, learning different parts of business, and now she was ready for a role that combined all of it. Her resume showed progression within the chaos. She got the interview, and she was one of the best hires I ever made. The point: context matters. If your path isn't obvious, explain it.

Cover letters are tricky. Honestly? Most of the time, I don't read them. If your resume doesn't grab me, a cover letter won't save you. But sometimes — maybe 20% of the time — a cover letter is the difference-maker. It's when someone shows they actually understand the role, the company, and why they're a fit. Not generic flattery, but real insight. "I saw you just launched X product, and I've spent the last three years solving exactly that problem at my current company" — that gets read. That gets remembered.

Here's the key: tailor your application without lying. Don't pretend you have experience you don't have. But do emphasize the experience that's relevant. If you're applying for a marketing role and you've done marketing, put that first. If you've done other things too, that's fine, but lead with what matters for this job. Use the language from the job posting. If they're looking for someone who can "drive cross-functional collaboration," and you've done that, say it. Don't use their exact words — that looks robotic — but show you understand what they need.

The biggest mistakes I see: typos and grammar errors. One typo and I'm wondering if you're careless or if you didn't care enough to proofread. Either way, it's a problem. Generic applications are another killer. When I can tell you sent the same resume to 50 companies without changing anything, I know you're not serious about this one. And overstating experience is the kiss of death. "Led a team of 10" when you actually managed one person who reported to you — I will find out, and when I do, I'm done.

Your LinkedIn profile should match your resume. Not word-for-word, but the same story. If your resume says you were a "Senior Marketing Manager" and your LinkedIn says "Marketing Coordinator," that's a red flag. If your resume lists accomplishments that don't show up anywhere on LinkedIn, I'm going to wonder which one is real. Keep them in sync. LinkedIn can be a bit more narrative and personal, but the core facts should line up.

Here's something people don't talk about: some of the best people I've hired had messy resumes. Gaps in employment, weird job titles, unconventional paths. But the substance was there. They could explain the gaps. They could show what they'd learned. They had real accomplishments, even if the presentation wasn't perfect. If you're one of those people, don't panic. A good resume gets you the interview, but a good interview gets you the job. If your resume is rough but your experience is solid, own it. Be ready to explain it. Most hiring managers will listen if you're honest.

The bottom line: your resume is your first impression. Make it count. Be clear, be specific, be honest, and be relevant. You don't need to be fancy. You just need to make it easy for someone to see why you're worth 30 more seconds of their time.

## Job Search Strategy: How to Not Lose Your Mind

## Job Searching While Employed: How to Do It Without Torpedoing Your Current Job

Here's the paradox: the best time to job search is when you already have a job. You have leverage. You're not desperate. You can be selective. You can negotiate from a position of strength. But it's also the trickiest situation you'll face, because now you're managing two jobs at once — the one you're trying to leave and the one you're trying to get. And if you screw this up, you can lose both.

Let's start with the obvious: be discreet. Don't use your work computer to search for jobs. Don't check job boards on your work phone. Don't take calls from recruiters at your desk. Don't tell your coworkers you're looking. I know this sounds paranoid, but it's not. Companies monitor email. People talk. And once word gets out that you're job hunting, your current employer's behavior changes. Suddenly you're not invited to meetings. Your projects get reassigned. Your boss starts documenting everything you do wrong. You go from being a valued employee to being a liability they're waiting to replace. Don't give them that ammunition.

A team member — smart, talented, been at his company for five years — started job searching and got sloppy about it. He'd take calls from recruiters in the bathroom. He'd update his LinkedIn profile during work hours. He mentioned to one person that he was "exploring options." That person told someone else. Within two weeks, his manager knew. Within a month, he was put on a performance improvement plan for things that had never been a problem before. He was trying to leave anyway, but they made it so uncomfortable that he left before he had another job lined up. He took a lower salary at the next place just to get out. All because he wasn't careful.

So here's how you do this right: schedule interviews early in the morning or late in the afternoon, before work or after. If you need to take an interview during the day, use a personal day or a half day. Tell your boss you have a doctor's appointment or a personal errand. It's not a lie — you're taking care of yourself. If you're interviewing at a company nearby, go during lunch. If it's farther away, take a half day. Most hiring managers understand that employed candidates need flexibility, and they'll work with you on timing.

Now, the question everyone asks: should you tell your current employer you're looking? The answer is almost always no. There are rare exceptions — if you have a really good relationship with your boss and you're leaving for a specific reason that's not about them, you might tell them. But even then, you're taking a risk. The default answer is: keep it to yourself until you have an offer. Once you have an offer, then you can tell them. Not before.

Here's where it gets tricky: references. When a new employer asks for references, they're going to want to talk to your current boss. And you don't want them to. So here's what you do: be honest about it. Tell the hiring manager, "I'm still employed, and I haven't told my current employer I'm looking. Can we use my previous manager instead, or can we wait to contact my current employer until we've made a decision?" Most hiring managers will respect this. They've been in your position. They know the risk. If they won't work with you on this, that's a red flag about how they treat employees. And you probably don't want to work there anyway.

The harder part is maintaining your performance at your current job while you're mentally checked out. And you will be mentally checked out. You're thinking about the interview you just had. You're wondering if they're going to call. You're imagining yourself in a new role. Meanwhile, your boss is asking you to lead a project that's going to take three months. Here's the thing: you still have to do it. You still have to show up. You still have to deliver. Not because you owe it to them, but because you owe it to yourself. If you start phoning it in, your performance drops, and that's going to show up in references. And it's going to affect your reputation. Do the work. Do it well. Leave on good terms. You never know when you're going to run into these people again.

Let me be clear about something: don't job search on company time. Don't spend your workday updating your resume or browsing job boards or taking calls from recruiters. That's not just unethical — it's stupid. You're using their resources to leave them. And if they find out, they have every right to be angry. Use your personal time. Use your lunch break. Use your evenings and weekends. Yes, it's exhausting. Yes, it sucks. But that's the price of doing this the right way.

Now, here's the scenario that keeps people up at night: you know you're leaving, but they don't. You're in the middle of a big project. Your boss is counting on you. Do you finish it, or do you bail? The answer is: you finish it. Or at least, you don't leave them hanging. If you're going to be there for another month or two, you see the project through. If you're leaving in two weeks and there's a six-month project, you document what you've done, you hand off what you can, and you make sure the next person has what they need to succeed. You don't sabotage the place on your way out. That's not professional, and it's not who you want to be.

Here's the thing about leaving: even if you hate your current job, even if your boss is terrible, even if the company is a dumpster fire — you still leave professionally. You give two weeks' notice. You offer to help with the transition. You don't burn bridges. Why? Because the world is small. Your boss might end up at your next company. Your coworker might be on the hiring committee somewhere down the line. Your reputation follows you. And more importantly, you want to be able to look yourself in the mirror. You want to know that you did the right thing, even when it would have been easier not to.

When you do give notice, keep it simple. "I've accepted a position elsewhere, and my last day will be [date]." Don't over-explain. Don't apologize. Don't get into a negotiation about staying. They'll either counter-offer or they won't. If they do, you've already made your decision — that's why you're leaving. Don't let them talk you into staying. If they don't counter-offer, you're done. Work your notice period, help with the transition, and move on.

One last thing: the moment you accept an offer somewhere else, you can relax a little. You're not sneaking around anymore. You're not worried about getting caught. You're just counting down the days until you start your new job. And that's a good feeling. But until that moment comes, stay disciplined. Stay discreet. Stay professional. The job search is a marathon, not a sprint, and the people who win are the ones who don't trip themselves up in the final stretch.

Let's be honest: job searching is brutal. It's rejection on repeat. It's silence. It's hope followed by disappointment. Most career advice glosses over this and tells you to "stay positive" and "network authentically" like you're not slowly going insane refreshing your email every five minutes. I'm not going to do that. Job searching is one of the most emotionally draining things you'll do in your career, and pretending otherwise doesn't help anyone.

Here's what you need to know: the numbers are not in your favor, and that's normal. You're going to apply to a lot of jobs. Most of them won't even get a response. Of the ones that do, maybe 10-20% will turn into interviews. Of those interviews, maybe 1 in 3 or 1 in 4 will turn into an offer. So if you're applying to 50 jobs, you might get 5-10 interviews, and maybe 1-2 offers. That's not failure. That's how it works. The people who don't understand this get discouraged after two weeks of searching and start making desperate decisions. Don't be that person.

You need a system. Not because systems are fun, but because without one, you'll lose track of where you've applied, who you've talked to, and what you said to them. I've seen candidates apply to the same company twice in a month because they forgot they'd already done it. I've seen people follow up with the wrong hiring manager because they didn't keep notes. Get a spreadsheet. Track the company, the job title, the date you applied, the contact person if you have one, and the date you should follow up. Add notes about what you learned in any conversations. This takes 10 minutes per application and saves you from looking like you don't care.

A candidate I met did this right. He was looking for a marketing role, and he applied to about 30 jobs over two months. But here's what made him different: he wasn't just blasting out resumes. He researched each company. He customized his cover letter. He tracked everything. When he got an interview, he followed up within 24 hours with a specific note about something they discussed. He applied consistently — not frantically, but steadily. He got 8 interviews and 2 offers. Another candidate applied to 200 jobs in three weeks. He was panicked. He sent generic cover letters. He didn't follow up. He got 2 interviews and no offers. Same market, same skill level. Different approach, completely different outcome.

The key is momentum. Not desperation, momentum. There's a difference. Desperation is applying to 50 jobs in a week because you're terrified. Momentum is applying to 5-10 jobs a week, consistently, for as long as it takes. Desperation shows in interviews —

you're too eager, you're willing to take anything, you seem unstable. Momentum shows differently. You're calm. You're selective. You're someone who's going to land somewhere good because you're being thoughtful about it. Hiring managers can smell the difference.

You're going to get rejected. A lot. And here's the thing that nobody tells you: even great candidates get rejected. I've rejected people I would have loved to hire because someone else was a slightly better fit. I've rejected people because the timing was wrong or the budget changed or we decided to go in a different direction. None of that was about them being bad. It was just how it worked out. When you get rejected, it's not personal. It's not a referendum on your worth. It's just a no. The sooner you accept that, the sooner you can move on to the next one without carrying the weight of it.

Here's where people mess up: they get desperate. They start applying to jobs they're not qualified for. They start lowballing themselves on salary. They start saying yes to interviews for jobs they don't actually want, just to have something to do. They start messaging people on LinkedIn they've never met, asking for jobs. And all of this desperation comes through. It makes you seem unstable. It makes hiring managers nervous. If you're this desperate now, what happens when things get hard at the job? So here's what you do instead: you set a boundary. You decide what you're actually looking for. You decide what salary you actually need. And you stick to it. If that means fewer applications, fine. Better to have 10 good conversations than 100 desperate ones.

But also — and this is important — take breaks. Job searching is exhausting. If you're spending eight hours a day applying to jobs and refreshing your email, you're going to burn out. You're going to get depressed. You're going to start making bad decisions. I've seen it happen. Someone searches hard for three weeks, gets burned out, stops looking, and then wonders why they're not getting anywhere. Instead, set a schedule. Maybe you spend two hours a day on job search. Maybe you do it in the morning and then move on with your day. Maybe you take weekends off. You're allowed to have a life while you're looking for a job. In fact, you should. It keeps you sane. It keeps you from seeming desperate in interviews.

Networking gets a bad rap because people do it wrong. They treat it like a transaction. They reach out to someone they haven't talked to in five years and immediately ask for a job. That's not networking. That's using people. Real networking is simpler: reach out to people you actually know. Tell them you're looking. Ask if they know anyone at companies you're interested in. Have actual conversations. If someone offers to introduce you to someone, take it. If someone asks you to coffee, go. These conversations often lead nowhere, and that's fine. But sometimes they lead somewhere. And even when they don't, you're building relationships. You're staying connected. You're reminding people you exist.

Informational interviews are underrated. If you're interested in a company or a role, reach out to someone who works there. Not the hiring manager — someone in the department or a peer role. Ask if they have 20 minutes to talk about what it's like to work there. Most people will say yes. Most people like talking about their job. And you'll learn things that aren't on the website. You'll learn about the culture, the challenges, the real day-to-day. And if you're a good fit, they might pass your name along to the hiring manager. But even if they don't, you've learned something. You've made a connection. You've shown initiative. That matters.

Here's what I want you to understand: even great people struggle to find jobs. I've hired incredibly talented people who took three months to find their next role. I've hired people who applied to 100 jobs before they got an offer. I've hired people who got rejected by companies they would have been perfect for. This isn't a reflection on them. It's just how the market works. There's luck involved. There's timing. There's the fact that hiring is inefficient and sometimes the wrong person gets the job. So if you're struggling, that doesn't mean you're not good enough. It means you're in a job search. And job searches are hard.

The people who succeed aren't the ones who are the most talented. They're the ones who stay organized, stay consistent, and don't let rejection destroy them. They're the ones who apply to jobs they actually want, follow up thoughtfully, and treat the search like a job itself. They're the ones who take breaks so they don't burn out.

They're the ones who network without being creepy about it. They're the ones who understand that this is a numbers game and a patience game and an emotional game all at once.

So here's your job search strategy: be systematic, be consistent, be selective, and be kind to yourself. Track your applications. Customize your materials. Follow up. Network genuinely. Take breaks. And remember that rejection is not about you. It's just part of the process. The right job is out there. You just have to be patient enough and organized enough to find it.

### Questions You Need to Ask (That Most Candidates Don't)

Most job seekers are terrified to ask tough questions during an interview. They think it'll hurt their chances. They think they should just smile, answer questions, and hope for an offer. They're wrong.

The candidates who impressed me most weren't the ones who had all the right answers. They were the ones who asked the right questions. Because asking good questions tells me you're thinking critically, you're not desperate, and you actually care about whether this job is a fit. It tells me you're someone who will push back when something doesn't make sense — and that's exactly the kind of person you want on your team.

Here are the questions you need to ask:

### "What happened to the last person in this role?"

This is the question that separates serious candidates from people just going through the motions. Listen carefully to the answer. If they say "Oh, she got promoted," that's great — it means there's growth. If they say "He moved on to something else" with no detail, dig deeper. Ask where he went and why. If they get vague or defensive, that's a red flag. If they say "We had to let him go" or "It didn't work out," ask why. Was it a performance issue? A personality clash? A mismatch between the job description and the actual role? The answer tells you everything about whether this job is what they're actually selling you.

### "What does success look like in the first 6 months?"

This is non-negotiable. If they can't answer this clearly, they don't know what they want from you. And if they don't know what they want, you'll never know if you're doing it right. Listen for specific metrics or outcomes, not vague statements like "fit in with the team" or "learn the systems." If they say something like "Close three new accounts" or "Ship the redesigned dashboard," that's concrete. If they're still being fuzzy after you ask, that's a problem. You'll be chasing a moving target.

**"What's the biggest challenge this team is facing right now?"**

This question does two things. First, it tells you what you're actually walking into. Second, it tells you whether the manager is being honest with you. If they say "We don't really have any challenges, everything's great," they're either lying or they're not paying attention. Every team has challenges. The good managers know what they are and they're thinking about how to solve them. If they tell you the real problem — "We're struggling to retain junior developers" or "Our product is losing market share to a competitor" — that's honesty. That's someone you can work with.

**"How do you handle conflict on the team?"**

Watch how they answer this. Do they give you a specific example? Do they talk about it as a normal part of work, or do they act like conflict is something that shouldn't happen? The best managers I've worked with see conflict as information. They address it directly, they don't let it fester, and they don't take sides without understanding both perspectives. If they say "We don't really have conflict here," they're either managing a team of robots or they're avoiding problems. Neither is good for you.

**"What's your management style, and how do you give feedback?"**

This matters because you're going to spend 40+ hours a week with this person. If they say "I'm pretty hands-off, I let people figure things out," ask what that looks like when someone's struggling. If they say "I'm very involved," ask how they balance that with giving people autonomy. The best answer is usually something like "I check in regularly, I'm clear about expectations, and I give feedback in the moment — both positive and negative." If they say they never give negative feedback, or they only do it in formal reviews, that's a problem. You want to know where you stand.

**"What does the career path look like from here?"**

Don't ask this like you're already planning your exit. Ask it like you're genuinely curious about where this role can take you. Listen to whether they have a real answer or if they're making it up on the spot. If they say "Well, you could move into management" or "You could move to a different team," ask them to give you an example of someone who did that. If they can't, that's telling. It means either nobody's moved up from this role, or they don't actually have a development plan for their team.

**"What would you change about this role if you could?"**

This is a sneaky question because it gets them to be honest about the job's weaknesses. If they say "Nothing, it's perfect," they're not being real with you. Every role has something that could be better. Maybe it's the tools, maybe it's the team structure, maybe it's the reporting lines. If they can articulate what they'd change and why, that tells you they're thinking about how to make things better. If they can't, they're either not paying attention or they don't care.

**"How often do we check in, and what does that look like?"**

This tells you about their management philosophy and whether you'll actually get feedback and support. If they say "We do monthly one-on-ones," that's not enough. If they say "We check in weekly, and I'm available if you need me," that's better. If they say "I do quick check-ins a few times a week, and we have a formal one-on-one every other week," that's someone who actually cares about their team's development. The frequency matters, but so does the tone. Are they checking in to help you succeed, or are they checking in to make sure you're not screwing up?

**"What does the career path look like from here?"**

Don't ask this like you're already planning your exit. Ask it like you're genuinely curious about where this role can take you. Listen to whether they have a real answer or if they're making it up on the spot. If they say "Well, you could move into management" or "You could move to a different team," ask them to give you an example of

37

someone who did that. If they can't, that's telling. It means either nobody's moved up from this role, or they don't actually have a development plan for their team.

**"What would you change about this role if you could?"**

This is a sneaky question because it gets them to be honest about the job's weaknesses. If they say "Nothing, it's perfect," they're not being real with you. Every role has something that could be better. Maybe it's the tools, maybe it's the team structure, maybe it's the reporting lines. If they can articulate what they'd change and why, that tells you they're thinking about how to make things better. If they can't, they're either not paying attention or they don't care.

**"How often do we check in, and what does that look like?"**

A candidate once asked me, "If I take this job and things aren't working out in three months, what would that look like? What would tell you it's not a fit?" Most candidates would never ask that. But this guy did. And I respected it immediately because it told me he was thinking about the relationship as a two-way street. He wasn't just hoping it would work out — he was being realistic about the possibility that it might not. I hired him on the spot. He turned out to be one of the best people I ever worked with.

Here's the thing about reading their answers: Pay attention to what they don't say as much as what they do. If you ask about challenges and they spend five minutes talking about how great everything is, they're either delusional or they're selling you a story. If you ask about conflict and they give you a vague answer, they're avoiding the question. If you ask about feedback and they talk about formal reviews instead of ongoing conversations, they're not going to help you grow. Listen for specifics, examples, and honesty. If you're getting generic corporate-speak, that's a red flag. If you're getting real answers from someone who's clearly thought about these things, that's someone worth working for.

**Evaluating Job Offers: It's Not Just About the Salary**

Here's what I see happen all the time: Someone gets a job offer. The salary number is higher than what they're making now, so they take it. Six months later, they're miserable. They're working 60-hour weeks, their manager is a nightmare, they haven't learned anything new, and they're stuck in a worse position than they were before. The money looked good on paper. Everything else was a disaster.

People take jobs based on salary because it's the easiest number to understand. It's concrete. It's immediate. But it's also the least important part of the equation if the rest of the job is broken. You can't spend money if you're too burned out to enjoy it. You can't build a career if you're working for someone who doesn't develop their people. And you definitely can't get ahead if you're spending all your energy just trying to survive.

When you get a job offer, you need to evaluate the whole package. Not just what they're paying you, but what you're actually getting for your time and your life.

### The Components You Need to Understand

Start with base salary, obviously. That's your floor. But then look at the bonus structure. Is it realistic? How many people actually hit their bonus targets? I've seen companies where the bonus is theoretically 20% of your salary, but nobody's hit it in three years because the targets are impossible. Ask about it. Ask what percentage of people in that role actually received their full bonus last year. If they can't answer that, that's a red flag.

Then there's equity. If they're offering you stock options or RSUs, you need to understand what that actually means. Is it worth anything? When does it vest? What's the strike price? I've seen people get excited about equity packages that are essentially worthless because the company's valuation is inflated or the vesting schedule is brutal. If you don't understand it, ask someone who does. Don't just nod and smile. Equity can be real money, but only if you understand the terms.

Benefits matter more than people think. Health insurance, retirement matching, life insurance — these aren't sexy, but they're real money. A company that matches 6% of your 401k is giving you an extra 6% of your salary. That adds up. And if you have a family, the health insurance quality matters. A high deductible plan that saves the company money but costs you thousands out of pocket is a pay cut, not a benefit.

PTO is another one people overlook. Some companies give you unlimited PTO, which sounds great until you realize nobody actually takes it because the culture doesn't support it. Other companies give you 15 days and actually encourage you to use them. Which one is better? The one where you actually get to rest. Ask about it. Ask how much PTO the person's manager takes. That'll tell you the real story.

Flexibility and remote work have become huge. If you're commuting an hour each way to an office, that's 10 hours a week of your life gone. That's not nothing. If the new job is remote or flexible, that's worth real money in terms of your time and sanity. If it's not, factor that in. Some people don't mind the commute. Most people do.

Growth opportunities are where long-term value lives. Will you learn new skills? Will you work with people who are better than you? Will you have a manager who actually develops you? These things don't show up in your paycheck, but they show up in your career five years from now. A job that pays 10% more but teaches you nothing is a step backward, even if it doesn't feel like it.

### The Story of Turning Down More Money

I got offered a job once that paid 30% more than what I was making. Thirty percent. That's real money. The company was bigger, more prestigious, and the title was better. On paper, it was a no-brainer.

But I asked the right questions. I talked to people who worked there. I learned that the manager had a reputation for being difficult, that the team had high turnover, and that people were expected to be available on weekends. The bonus structure was aggressive but rarely paid out. The equity was diluted. And the commute was brutal.

I turned it down. My current manager matched most of the salary increase, and I stayed where I was. That decision saved me years of frustration. The person who took that job? He lasted 18 months and then had to rebuild his reputation because he'd burned out and started making mistakes. The 30% raise cost him more than it was worth.

**Short-Term vs. Long-Term Value**

Think about what this job is actually worth to you over the next three to five years. A job that pays well but doesn't teach you anything is a dead end. A job that pays less but puts you in a position to earn significantly more later is an investment. A job that destroys your health or your relationships is costing you money you don't even realize.

I've seen people take jobs that looked good for two years and then realized they'd hit a ceiling. They'd learned everything they could learn, they weren't growing, and they were stuck. Meanwhile, someone who took a slightly lower-paying job at a company with better development opportunities had moved up twice and was now making significantly more.

The money you make in year one matters. But the trajectory matters more. Where will you be in three years if you take this job? Will you be more valuable? Will you have learned new skills? Will you have connections that open doors? Or will you be in the same place, just older?

**The Hidden Costs of Toxic Workplaces**

Here's what people don't talk about: the cost of working somewhere toxic. It's not just the stress, though that's real. It's the health impact. High blood pressure, sleep problems, anxiety — these things are expensive. They're also permanent. You can't get those years back.

It's also career stagnation. When you're in survival mode, you're not learning. You're not building relationships. You're not doing your best work. And when you finally leave, you've lost time. You could have been somewhere else, building skills and reputation, instead of just trying to get through the day.

And then there's the reputational damage. If you work somewhere toxic, you start to absorb that toxicity. You make mistakes because you're stressed. You burn bridges because you're frustrated. You leave that job damaged in ways that take years to recover from. I've seen people take jobs for money and then spend the next five years trying to rebuild their professional reputation.

The math is simple: A job that pays 20% more but costs you your health and your career momentum is a bad deal. Full stop.

**Using Competing Offers Ethically**

If you have multiple offers, that's leverage. Use it. But use it honestly. Don't bluff. Don't tell a company you have another offer if you don't. Don't exaggerate what the other offer is. That's how you burn bridges and get a reputation as someone who's not trustworthy.

But if you genuinely have another offer, you can use it. You can say, "I'm really interested in this role, but I have another offer that's offering X. Is there any flexibility on salary or benefits?" Most companies will work with you if they want you. Some won't. If they won't, that tells you something about how they value people.

The key is to be honest about it. Don't make it a threat. Make it a conversation. "I want to work here, but I need to make sure the package makes sense for me." That's reasonable. That's professional. That's how adults negotiate.

**Asking for Time to Decide**

When you get an offer, you don't have to decide immediately. Most companies will give you a few days. Some will give you a week. Ask for what you need. "I'm very interested in this opportunity. Can I have until Friday to think it through?" That's a reasonable request.

Use that time wisely. Talk to people who work there. Research the company. Sleep on it. Your gut will tell you things your brain hasn't figured out yet. If you're excited but nervous, that's normal. If you're excited but something feels off, pay attention to that.

How much time is reasonable? Three to five business days is standard. A week is pushing it. Two weeks is too long — they'll assume you're not interested. But don't let anyone pressure you into deciding on the spot. That's a red flag in itself. Good companies understand that you need time to make a good decision.

**Trust Your Gut, Even When the Numbers Look Good**

Here's the thing I've learned: Your instincts are usually right. If the money looks great but something feels off about the company or the manager or the role, that feeling is probably based on something real. You've picked up on signals that your conscious mind hasn't fully processed yet.

I've ignored my gut before. I've taken jobs because the numbers were good, even though I had a bad feeling about it. Every single time, I regretted it. The bad feeling was right. There was something wrong that I couldn't quite articulate, but it was there.

So when you're evaluating an offer, pay attention to how you feel. Do you feel excited about the work? Do you feel good about the people? Do you trust the manager? Do you believe what they're telling you? If the answer to any of those is no, that's important information. No amount of money is worth spending 40 hours a week somewhere that doesn't feel right.

The best job offer isn't the one with the biggest number. It's the one that makes sense for your whole life — your career, your health, your growth, and your sanity. Evaluate the whole package. Ask the hard questions. Trust your gut. And then make a decision you can live with.

Here's the truth: preparation shows respect. It shows you're serious. It separates the candidates who are mass-applying to every job posting from the ones who actually want to work somewhere. And in a competitive job market, that difference matters. A lot.

If you're looking for work, you need to interview them as hard as they're interviewing you. Because a bad employer will waste years of your life, and you won't get those years back.

**Red Flags During the Interview**

Pay attention to how they treat you before you're hired. That's the best version of themselves you're going to see.

Early in my career, I interviewed at a company where the president was 30 minutes late, didn't apologize, and spent the first ten minutes on his phone. Then he asked me three questions, barely listened to my answers, and wrapped it up in 15 minutes. He offered me the job the next day.

I should have run. Instead, I took it. And guess what? That's exactly how he managed. Late to meetings, distracted, uninterested in what anyone had to say. I lasted one year.

Watch for these warning signs:

- **They can't tell you what success looks like.** If they're vague about expectations or metrics, they don't know what they want. You'll never win because the target keeps moving.
- **They badmouth the person who left.** If they trash their last employee in the interview, they'll trash you when you leave. Good employers talk about what they learned from past hires, not how terrible everyone was.
- **The team looks miserable.** If you meet the team and everyone seems exhausted, distracted, or unwilling to make eye contact, believe what you're seeing. I've hired people into toxic teams and watched them burn out in months.
- **They're in a huge rush to hire.** Desperation means something's wrong. Either they can't keep people, or they're so disorganized they didn't plan ahead. Either way, you're walking into chaos.

### How to Succeed in Your First 90 Days

Once you take the job, the first three months determine everything. I've seen great hires fail because they didn't do these things:

**Ask questions early.** The people who succeed are the ones who admit what they don't know and ask for help in the first few weeks. The ones who struggle are the ones who fake it, hoping they'll figure it out. They don't.

**Deliver something small and visible.** Don't wait for the big project. Find something you can complete in your first two weeks and do it well. It builds trust and buys you patience for when you need it later.

**Pay attention to the culture.** Every workplace has unwritten rules. Does your boss prefer email or face-to-face? Do people work through lunch or take breaks? Is it okay to push back in meetings? Watch what successful people do and follow their lead.

One of my hires ignored all of this. He spent his first month redesigning processes nobody asked him to touch, skipped team meetings because he was "too busy," and never asked a single question. By week six, the team wanted him gone. He thought he was being proactive. He was actually being arrogant.

### When to Have the Hard Conversation

If something's not working, say it early. I've lost good people because they stayed quiet until they were so frustrated they quit.

A team member was drowning under her workload but never said anything. She thought asking for help would make her look weak. By the time she finally spoke up, she'd already accepted another job. If she'd told me two months earlier, I could have fixed it.

If you need to have a tough conversation with your manager, do it this way:

• Be specific. Don't say "I'm overwhelmed." Say "I have five projects due this week and I can't do all of them well. Can we prioritize?"

• Offer solutions. Don't just complain. Come with ideas. "I think if we pushed Project X to next week, I could deliver Y and Z on time."

• Pick the right time. Don't ambush them in the hallway. Ask for 15 minutes and tell them what you want to discuss.

Most managers want to help. But we can't fix what we don't know about.

### When It's Time to Leave

I've watched people stay in jobs that were killing them because they felt loyal, or scared, or thought it would get better. It rarely does.

You should leave when:

### Protecting Yourself During the Hiring Process

Now let's talk about something that matters just as much as knowing when to leave: protecting yourself when you're being hired. Because I've seen good people get burned by companies that seemed legitimate right up until they weren't.

### Get It in Writing Before You Quit

This is non-negotiable. Do not quit your current job until you have a written offer from the new company. Not a verbal agreement. Not a handshake. Not a promise from your future boss. A written offer with a start date, salary, title, and benefits clearly spelled out.

A candidate named David got a verbal offer over the phone. He was excited, gave his two weeks' notice, and told everyone at his current job he was leaving. Three days later, the new company called back. "We need to push your start date back six months due to budget constraints." He was already out of a job. He ended up taking a contract position at a lower rate just to pay his bills. A written offer would have protected him.

**Understand What You're Signing**

Before you sign anything, read it. I mean actually read it, not just skim it. Pay attention to:

• **Non-compete clauses.** These restrict where you can work after you leave. Some are reasonable (you can't go work for a direct competitor for six months). Some are insane (you can't work in your entire industry for two years within 50 miles). If it's unreasonable, push back. Many companies will negotiate this.

• **Non-solicitation agreements.** This usually means you can't recruit your company's employees or clients after you leave. That's fair. But make sure you understand the scope. Does it apply forever, or just for a year?

• **Intellectual property clauses.** Some companies claim ownership of anything you create while employed, even on your own time. That's overreach. Make sure it's limited to work-related projects created during work hours.

If you don't understand something, ask. If they won't explain it, that's a red flag. A legitimate company will be happy to clarify.

**Background Checks and What Can Go Wrong**

Most companies do background checks. That's normal. But things can go wrong. I've seen candidates lose offers because of errors on their credit report or a case of mistaken identity in the criminal database. Before you accept an offer contingent on a background check, pull your own. Check your credit report. Search your name in court records. If there's something that might come up, address it proactively with the company. "I want to make sure you're aware that I had a traffic ticket in 2015 that might show up." Transparency beats surprises.

**Salary Negotiations: Don't Play Yourself**

Here's what I see happen: A company asks, "What's your salary expectation?" and the candidate panics and throws out a number.

Then the company counters with something lower, and the candidate takes it because they're afraid to negotiate.

Do your research first. Use Glassdoor, Levels.fyi, PayScale, and industry reports to find out what the role actually pays in your market. Know your number before the conversation starts. And when they ask what you want, you have options: You can give a range ("Based on my research and experience, I'm looking for $85,000 to $95,000"), you can deflect ("I'm flexible depending on the full package"), or you can ask them first ("What's the budgeted range for this role?"). Most of the time, they'll tell you if you ask directly.

### The Full Compensation Package Matters

Salary is one number. But it's not the only number. Before you say yes, understand:

- Base salary
- Bonus structure (is it guaranteed, or is it "up to" a certain amount?)
- Stock options or equity (if applicable)
- Health insurance (what's the premium, deductible, and out-of-pocket max?)
- 401(k) match
- PTO (days per year, and can you actually take it?)
- Remote work flexibility
- Professional development budget
- Signing bonus (if applicable)

I've seen people accept jobs that looked good on paper but had terrible health insurance or no 401(k) match. That costs you real money over time. Ask for the full benefits package in writing. Compare it to what you have now. Sometimes a lower salary with better benefits is actually a better deal.

### Red Flags During the Offer Stage

If any of these things happen, slow down:

- **Pressure to start immediately.** "We need you to start Monday" when you just got the offer on Friday. Legitimate companies understand you need time to transition. If they're pushing hard, they're either desperate or they don't respect boundaries.

• **Vague terms.** "We'll work out the details once you start." No. Get the details now. If they won't pin down salary, title, or responsibilities before you start, they're leaving room to change things on you.

• **Constant changes to the offer.** First it was $80,000, then it's $75,000, then they want to add a probationary period. Every time you think you're done negotiating, something new comes up. This is a sign they don't know what they're doing or they're testing how much they can push you around.

• **No written confirmation.** If everything's still verbal after multiple conversations, that's a problem. Get it in writing.

### How to Gracefully Decline

Sometimes after all this, you realize it's not the right fit. Maybe the role changed, or the team seems toxic, or the money just isn't there. You can say no. You don't need to burn the bridge.

"Thank you for the offer. I've given it serious thought, and I don't think it's the right fit for me at this time. I appreciate the opportunity and hope we can stay in touch." That's it. You don't owe them a detailed explanation. You don't need to justify your decision. A simple, professional decline is enough.

### If They Rescind the Offer

This happens sometimes. Budget gets cut, the role gets eliminated, or they hire someone else. It sucks, but it happens. If it happens before you've quit your current job, you're protected. If it happens after, you have options: You can ask if there's another role available, you can ask for severance, or you can move on. Don't panic. You still have your current job (assuming you didn't quit early). Use this time to figure out what went wrong and whether you want to work with this company at all.

### Trust Your Gut

Here's the thing about all of this: If something feels off during the hiring process, it probably is. I've ignored my gut before and regretted it. A company that's disorganized during hiring is usually disorganized once you're there. A hiring manager who's evasive about compensation is usually evasive about feedback and growth too.

You're not being paranoid by asking questions and protecting yourself. You're being smart. This is a business transaction. Treat it like one. Get everything in writing, understand what you're signing, and don't be afraid to walk away if it's not right. There will be other jobs. There's only one you.

• **You've stopped learning.** If you're doing the same thing you were doing a year ago and nobody's investing in your growth, you're stalling.

• **Your manager doesn't have your back.** If they throw you under the bus, take credit for your work, or won't fight for you when it matters, get out.

• **The company's in denial.** If leadership is pretending everything's fine while the ship is sinking, don't go down with it. I've seen too many good people stay out of loyalty and end up unemployed when the company folds.

• **It's affecting your health.** If you're losing sleep, snapping at your family, or dreading Monday on Saturday afternoon, no job is worth that.

I stayed too long at a job once because I kept thinking it would improve. It didn't. I left two years later than I should have, burned out and bitter. Don't do that.

### The Bottom Line

You're not lucky to have a job. They're lucky to have you. Interview them. Ask hard questions. And if it's not right, walk away.

Your career is long. One bad job won't ruin it. But staying in a bad job for too long might.

**If you're being hired:** Know your number. The one you'll accept, and the one that makes you walk. Write them down before the conversation starts.

**If you're negotiating:** Be transparent. Say what you want and why. Listen to what they say. Then decide.

I've been cheap and lost great people. I've played games and wasted weeks. I've taken jobs I shouldn't have because I didn't ask for what I was worth. All of it was avoidable.

Pay people fairly or don't hire them. Know your worth or don't negotiate. And if you can't agree on money, shake hands and walk away with respect.

Better to walk away over money than to start a relationship built on resentment.

## If You've Been Fired or Laid Off: How to Handle It in Interviews

Getting fired or laid off is one of the scariest moments in a job search. You're already vulnerable — you've lost income, your confidence is shaken, and now you have to explain it to strangers who are deciding whether to hire you. The fear is real. But here's what I want you to know: it's manageable, and good employers understand that sometimes things don't work out.

First, understand the difference between being laid off and being fired. A layoff is a business decision — the company is restructuring, downsizing, or eliminating your role. There's no shame in that. It happens to good people all the time. Being fired for performance is trickier, but it's not a career death sentence. The difference matters in how you frame it, but honesty matters more than framing.

When someone asks "Why did you leave your last job?" — and they will — you need an answer that's honest but strategic. Don't lie. Lying will come back to haunt you, and reference checks will expose it. But you also don't need to volunteer every painful detail or trash your former employer. Here's the difference:

**Bad answer:** "My boss was terrible and didn't appreciate my work. The whole company was a mess, and I couldn't stand working there anymore."

**Good answer:** "The role wasn't the right fit for what the company needed, and we both realized that pretty quickly. I learned a lot about what I do well and what I need in a work environment going forward. I'm looking for something where I can contribute more directly to [specific area]."

If you were laid off, be straightforward: "The company went through a restructuring and my position was eliminated. It was a business decision, not performance-related. I'm looking for my next opportunity where I can [specific value you bring]."

If you were fired for performance, take responsibility without self-flagellation. "I wasn't performing at the level the role required. I've spent time understanding why — [specific thing you learned about yourself] — and I've worked on that. Here's what I'm doing differently now." Then show evidence. Did you take a course? Get feedback from a mentor? Work on a project that proved you'd addressed the issue? Bring that.

The key is this: don't make excuses, but do show growth. A good employer knows that sometimes people land in the wrong role or the wrong company. What they want to see is that you learned something and you're not going to repeat the same pattern. They want to know you're self-aware enough to recognize what went wrong and honest enough to talk about it.

Here's the truth: if an employer holds a firing against you permanently, they're not the right employer anyway. The ones worth working for understand that careers aren't linear. They've been fired or laid off themselves, or they've managed people who have. They know that a single bad fit doesn't define someone's entire career. What defines you is how you handle it — whether you blame everyone else or whether you own your part and move forward smarter.

So when you're in that interview and the question comes up, breathe. Tell the truth. Show what you learned. And remember: you're not damaged goods. You're someone who's been tested and came out the other side ready to do better.

6

# Onboarding Without the Fluff: Setting Expectations Early

Most onboarding is a waste of time — death by PowerPoint, a stack of policies nobody reads, free mugs and empty promises. You want people productive, not just present.

I've been through ineffective onboarding as an employee, and I've run ineffective onboarding as a manager. The worst was at a company where new hires spent their entire first week in a conference room learning about company history, values, and policies. By day three, everyone was glazed over. By day five, they'd forgotten everything.

Then they got to their desks and had no idea what they were actually supposed to do.

That's not onboarding. That's hazing.

Real onboarding is about getting people productive as fast as possible while setting them up for long-term success. It's about clarity, not ceremony.

## The Essentials of Real Onboarding
### Start Before Day One

Send them a clear message: "Here's what winning looks like. Here's what will get you fired." No surprises.

The best onboarding starts before the first day. As soon as

someone accepts your offer, send them a welcome packet that includes:

• A clear description of what success looks like in their first 30, 60, and 90 days

• An overview of the team, the mission, and how their role fits in

• The non-negotiables: What behaviors or performance issues will get them fired

• Practical information: Where to park, what to wear, who they'll be working with

I also sent new hires a short video from me explaining what they should expect. Not corporate propaganda, but real talk: "Here's what's great about this team. Here's what's hard. Here's what I expect from you."

This does two things: It gets them excited, and it weeds out people who realize this isn't the right fit before they even start.

A candidate once declined an offer after receiving the welcome packet because they realized the pace and expectations weren't what they wanted. That's a win. Better to find out before they start than after.

### Assign a Buddy — Not a Babysitter

Pair them with someone who knows the ropes and actually cares, not just someone who's been there longest.

The buddy system works, but only if you do it right. Don't just assign the person who's been there longest or who happens to sit nearby. Assign someone who:

• Is good at their job (you want the new hire learning from someone competent)

• Is patient and willing to help (not everyone is)

• Represents the culture you want (not the culture you have)

I made it clear to buddies that this is part of their job, not a favor. And I gave them guidance: "Your job is to help them navigate the first few weeks. Answer their questions, introduce them to people, and let me know if you see any red flags."

I also checked in with both the new hire and the buddy regularly. "How's it going? What's working? What's not?"

The buddy system fails when it's just a name on paper. It works when it's an actual relationship with clear expectations.

### Set Short-Term Goals

• Shadow these five people and write up what you learned
• Deliver this small project
• Have one-on-ones with everyone on the team

The goals should be challenging but achievable. You want them to feel like they're contributing, not just observing.

In one case, a new hire in her first 30 days was supposed to audit our current process and make recommendations for improvement. It was a real project with real impact, but it was also contained enough that she couldn't do too much damage if she got it wrong.

She did excellent work. Her recommendations were solid, and implementing them became her first major project. She felt valuable from day one, and I got useful work out of her immediately.

### Be Brutally Honest

Tell them the hardest parts of the job. Don't sugarcoat. People respect candor, not spin.

On day one, I had a conversation with every new hire that went something like this:

"Here's what you need to know about this job. The best part is X. The hardest part is Y. The thing that drives most people crazy is Z. If you can handle those things, you'll do great. If you can't, this probably isn't the right fit."

I told them about the parts of the culture that are challenging. I tell them about the projects that failed. I tell them about the mistakes I've made.

This does two things: It builds trust (because I'm being honest), and it sets realistic expectations (so they're not blindsided later).

One of my hires heard this on her first day: "The hardest part of this job is that priorities change constantly. You'll start working on something, and then we'll pivot because the market shifted or a client need changed. If you need stability and predictability, you're going to struggle here."

She appreciated the honesty. And when we did pivot a few weeks later, she rolled with it because she'd been warned.

### Feedback Is Oxygen

Don't wait for the 90-day review. Give feedback daily, weekly — whenever it matters. Course-correct in real time. Silence isn't kindness; it's negligence.

The biggest mistake managers make in onboarding is waiting too long to give feedback. They don't want to overwhelm the new hire or seem too critical, so they stay silent.

Then at the 90-day review, they dump a bunch of feedback on the person, who's blindsided because they thought everything was fine.

That's not fair. If someone's doing something wrong, tell them immediately. If they're doing something right, tell them that too.

I did quick check-ins with new hires every few days for the first month. "How's it going? What's confusing? What's going well?" And I give them real-time feedback: "That report you sent was great. Next time, include more data to back up your recommendations." Or: "You were late to the team meeting this morning. That's not okay. I need you here on time."

Small course corrections early prevent big problems later.

### Create a 30-60-90 Day Plan

This is the roadmap for their first three months. It should include:

### First 30 Days: Learn

• Understand the team, the mission, and the basics of the role
• Complete initial training
• Deliver one small project to prove they can execute
• Build relationships with key stakeholders

### Days 31-60: Contribute

• Take on more responsibility
• Start working independently on projects
• Identify areas for improvement or innovation
• Demonstrate they can handle the core responsibilities of the role

### Days 61-90: Own

• Fully own their area of responsibility
• Deliver results without hand-holding

• Start mentoring or helping others

• Show they're ready to take on bigger challenges

At the end of 90 days, you should know whether this person is going to work out. If they've hit their goals and demonstrated the behaviors you need, great. If not, you have a decision to make.

## What to Avoid

### Endless Paperwork

If you're making them fill out forms for a week, you're doing it wrong.

Yes, there's administrative work that has to be done. But don't make it the focus of their first week. Get the paperwork done efficiently and move on to the real work.

I've seen companies where new hires spend days filling out forms, watching compliance videos, and sitting through HR presentations. By the time they get to their actual job, they're bored and demoralized.

Do the administrative stuff, but don't let it dominate. Get them doing real work as fast as possible.

### Cultural Indoctrination

Skip the "we're a family" speeches. Instead, share war stories, real wins and losses. Show, don't tell.

Don't tell people about your culture. Show them.

Instead of a presentation about your values, have them sit in on real meetings. Let them see how decisions get made, how conflicts get resolved, how the team actually works.

Share real stories: "Here's a project that went really well and why." "Here's a project that failed and what we learned." "Here's a tough decision we had to make and how we made it."

That's how people learn your culture — by seeing it in action, not by reading about it in a slide deck.

### Assuming They'll Figure It Out

Some managers go too far in the other direction and give new hires no structure at all. "Just jump in and figure it out."

That's not onboarding. That's abandonment.

Even experienced hires need guidance on how your specific team works. Don't assume they'll figure it out on their own.

## The Onboarding Test

You know if your onboarding is working when, at the end of 30 days, you ask the new hire:

- Do you understand what success looks like in this role?
- Do you know who to go to when you need help?
- Do you feel like you're contributing?
- Is there anything about the job that surprised you (in a bad way)?

If they can't answer yes to the first three questions, your onboarding needs work. If they say yes to the fourth question, you weren't transparent enough upfront.

Onboarding is your first real test as a leader. Set clear expectations, communicate openly, and treat your new hire like a professional. They'll rise to the occasion — or you'll know quickly if the fit isn't right.

7

# When Good Hires Go Bad: Managing Underperformance

No one bats a thousand. Even your best-looking hires will sometimes disappoint you. The key isn't to panic the first time someone stumbles. The key is to spot the slide and act before it turns into a serious problem.

I've had great employees suddenly start underperforming. I've had people I thought were solid turn out to be mediocre. And I've had people I was ready to fire turn things around and become stars.

The key is knowing the difference between a temporary slump and a permanent problem — and acting accordingly.

**What Underperformance Really Looks Like**

Underperformance isn't always obvious. It's not just missing deadlines or making mistakes. Sometimes it's subtler:

• **Missing deadlines — repeatedly, not just once during crunch time.** Everyone misses a deadline occasionally. But if someone's consistently late, that's a pattern.

• **Sloppy work, lack of attention to detail.** Work that used to be solid is now full of errors. They're not checking their work or they don't seem as invested anymore.

• **Energy drops. Engagement drops. They're checked out.** They used to be engaged in meetings, asking questions, contributing ideas. Now they're quiet, distracted, going through the motions.

• **People around them start expressing concerns, even if you don't want to hear it.** Other team members are picking up their slack or dealing with the consequences of their mistakes.

The tricky part is that underperformance often starts small. One missed deadline. One sloppy report. One meeting where they seem distracted. It's easy to dismiss as a bad day or a busy week.

But if you see multiple signs over multiple weeks, you have a problem.

### Why Good Hires Go Bad

Before you jump to "they're lazy" or "they don't care," consider what might be causing the underperformance:

### Personal Issues

Health problems, family stress, mental health struggles. Sometimes good employees hit rough patches in their personal lives that affect their work.

### Burnout

They've been working too hard for too long, and they're running on empty.

### Unclear Expectations

Maybe you think you've been clear about what you need, but they're confused or working on the wrong things.

### Poor Fit

The job has changed, or they've changed, and it's no longer a good match.

### Lack of Skills

They're in over their head and don't know how to ask for help.

### Loss of Motivation

They're bored, unchallenged, or don't see a future here.

Your job is to figure out which of these is the problem — because the solution is different for each one.

### What to Do About It
### Don't Avoid the Conversation

Ignoring problems doesn't make them go away. Address them early, before things get worse.

The moment you notice underperformance, address it. Don't wait for the next review cycle. Don't hope it'll get better on its own. Don't avoid the conversation because it's uncomfortable.

Early in my career, an employee's work started slipping. I noticed it, but I told myself he was just having a bad week. Then another bad week. Then another. By the time I finally addressed it, the problem had been going on for two months and the rest of the team was frustrated.

If I'd addressed it after the first week, we could have fixed it quickly. Instead, I let it fester.

## Be Direct and Respectful

"I've noticed your work has been slipping. This isn't personal. I need you to get back on track, or we're going to have a more serious problem."

A script I used:

"I need to talk to you about your performance. Over the past [timeframe], I've noticed [specific examples]. This isn't the standard I expect from you, and it's not the standard you've shown me in the past. What's going on?"

Then shut up and listen.

Sometimes they'll tell you something you didn't know. "I've been dealing with a family health issue and I'm not sleeping." "I'm overwhelmed and I don't know how to prioritize." "I'm confused about what you actually want from me."

Sometimes they'll get defensive. "I don't think my work is slipping." "Everyone else is having the same problems." "You're being unfair."

Either way, you've started the conversation. And that's the first step.

## Get Specific

Vague feedback is useless. Point to numbers, missed goals, and real examples.

Don't say: "Your work hasn't been great lately."

Say: "You missed the deadline on the Johnson project by three days. The report you submitted for the Smith account had multiple errors that the client caught. And you've been late to three team meetings in the past two weeks."

Specific feedback is harder to argue with and easier to act on.

I kept a running document of performance issues for every employee. Not because I'm looking to build a case against them, but because I want to be able to point to specific examples when we have performance conversations.

Vague feedback lets people off the hook. Specific feedback creates accountability.

### Give a Real Chance

Set a timeline for improvement. Thirty days. Concrete goals. Clear expectations.

After you've identified the problem, work with them to create an improvement plan:

"Here's what needs to change: [specific behaviors or outcomes]. Here's the timeline: [30 days, 60 days, whatever makes sense]. Here's how we'll measure success: [specific metrics or milestones]. And here's the support I'll provide: [training, resources, check-ins]."

Put it in writing. Have them sign it. Schedule regular check-ins to track progress.

This isn't about being punitive. It's about being clear. They know exactly what's expected, and you both know whether they're meeting those expectations.

One employee's work had become consistently late and sloppy. We created a 30-day improvement plan with specific goals: All deadlines met, all work reviewed for errors before submission, proactive communication if problems arise.

We checked in weekly. For the first two weeks, he struggled. By week three, he was hitting his marks. By week four, he was back to his old standard.

The improvement plan worked because it was specific, time-bound, and we both committed to it.

### Check Yourself

Are your expectations clear? Is this a support issue, or a motivation issue?

Sometimes underperformance is actually a management problem.

Ask yourself:

• Have I been clear about what I expect?
• Have I given them the resources and support they need?
• Am I asking them to do something they're not equipped to do?
• Have I created an environment where they can succeed?

An employee who I once thought was underperforming turned out to be responding to my own poor management. I'd been giving her conflicting priorities and changing direction constantly. She wasn't underperforming — she was trying to hit a moving target.

**When Enough is Enough**

If they can't (or won't) turn it around, you know what comes next. Don't drag it out. You're not running a rehabilitation program.

You know it's time to move on when:

• You've been clear about expectations and they're still not meeting them
• You've provided support and resources and it's not helping
• The improvement plan timeline has passed and there's no improvement
• They're not taking responsibility or showing any willingness to change
• The rest of the team is suffering because of their underperformance

At that point, you're not helping them by keeping them around. You're just prolonging the inevitable and hurting your team in the process.

I kept an underperformer for six months longer than I should have because I felt bad. He was a nice guy, he was trying, but he just couldn't do the job at the level we needed.

During those six months, the rest of the team had to pick up his slack. Two people got burned out. One person quit. And the underperformer himself was miserable because he knew he was failing.

When I finally let him go, everyone was relieved — including him. He found a job that was a better fit, and the team could finally function properly again.

**The Underperformance Decision Tree**
A simple framework for deciding what to do:
**Is this a new problem or a pattern?**
• New problem → Have a conversation, provide support, see if it resolves
• Pattern → Move to formal improvement plan
**Is the person aware there's a problem?**
• Not aware → You haven't been clear enough; fix your communication
• Aware → They're either unable or unwilling to fix it
**Are they trying to improve?**
• Yes → Give them time and support
• No → Time to move on
**Is the rest of the team suffering?**
• Yes → You need to act faster
• No → You have more time to work with them
**The Bottom Line on Underperformance**
Managing underperformance is one of the hardest parts of leadership because it requires you to balance compassion with accountability.

You want to give people a fair chance. You want to support them. But you also have a responsibility to your team and your mission.

The key is to act quickly, be clear, provide real support, and know when to cut your losses.

Don't let underperformance drag on. It's not fair to anyone — not to you, not to the team, and not to the person who's struggling.

8

# The Right Way to Fire: Rip the Band-Aid Off

Firing is the job everyone dreads. If you don't, you're probably a sociopath. But dragging your feet helps no one. Bad fits hurt teams, drain resources, and make your life difficult.

I've fired people for performance issues, for toxic behavior, for dishonesty, and for layoffs that had nothing to do with their performance. Every single time, it was hard. But every single time, it was the right call.

The worst firings I've done were the ones I delayed. The best ones were the ones I did quickly and cleanly once I knew it was over.

### How to Fire With Respect (and Minimal Drama)
### Don't Wait

The moment you know it's over, act. Waiting won't turn things around.

There's a moment in every failing employment relationship where you know it's not going to work. Maybe they've failed the improvement plan. Maybe they've done something unforgivable. Maybe the fit is just wrong and it's not getting better.

When you reach that moment, act.

Early in my career, I'd agonize over firing decisions. I'd give people extra chances, extend improvement plans, hope that somehow things would magically get better. They never did.

All I accomplished by waiting was:

• Prolonging everyone's discomfort

• Giving the rest of the team more time to get frustrated

• Making the eventual firing more awkward because we'd dragged it out so long

Now, when I know it's over, I move quickly. Not impulsively — I make sure I've documented everything and consulted with HR and legal. But once the decision is made, I act.

**Keep It Short and Unemotional**

"This isn't working out. Today's your last day." Don't turn it into a therapy session.

The firing conversation should be short. Ten minutes, max. The structure:

**1. State the decision clearly:** "I've made the decision to let you go. Today is your last day."

**2. Give a brief reason:** "We've talked about your performance issues multiple times, and despite the improvement plan, you haven't met the standards we need."

**3. Explain the logistics:** "HR will walk you through the paperwork. You'll receive [severance/final paycheck/whatever]. Your benefits continue through [date]."

**4. End the conversation:** "I wish you the best. HR is waiting to meet with you now."

That's it. Don't apologize. Don't get into a debate about whether the decision is fair. Don't let them talk you into giving them another chance.

The decision is made. This conversation is just informing them of it.

In one case, I let a firing conversation turn into a 45-minute debate. The employee argued with every point I made, tried to negotiate for more time, and got emotional. I felt terrible and started second-guessing myself.

But the conversation didn't change anything. He still got fired. All I did was make it more painful for both of us.

Now I kept it short. It's kinder that way.

**Be Honest, Not Brutal**

They deserve to hear the truth, but they don't need a character assassination.

There's a balance between being honest and being cruel.

Honest: "Your performance hasn't met our standards despite multiple conversations and an improvement plan."

Cruel: "You're just not good enough for this job and you never were."

Honest: "Your behavior toward colleagues has been unprofessional and created a difficult environment."

Cruel: "Everyone on the team dislikes you and thinks you're problematic."

Tell them the truth about why they're being fired, but don't pile on. This is already a hard moment. Don't make it worse by being unnecessarily harsh.

**Document Everything**

Not for drama — for protection. If you can't point to facts, you're not ready.

Before you fire anyone, make sure you have documentation:
• Performance reviews showing the issues
• Records of conversations about the problems
• The improvement plan and evidence they didn't meet it
• Any incidents of misconduct or policy violations
• Emails or other written communication about the issues

This isn't about building a legal case (though it might become one). It's about making sure you're being fair and that you can defend your decision if challenged.

One employee claimed they were blindsided by being fired. But when I pulled out the documentation — three performance reviews noting the same issues, two improvement plans, multiple documented conversations — it was clear they'd had plenty of warning.

Documentation protects you and ensures you're being fair.

**Have a Witness**

Never fire someone alone. Have HR or another manager in the room.

This protects both you and the employee. It ensures there's a witness to what was said, and it provides support if the conversation gets difficult.

Early in my career, I fired someone without a witness. He later claimed I'd said things I never said and promised things I never promised. It was his word against mine, and it created a mess.

Now I always have someone else in the room.

### Protect the Team

Announce it quickly and privately. Don't let rumors fester.

After you fire someone, you need to tell the team. Not all the details, but enough that they understand what happened and can move forward.

I usually send a brief email or have a quick team meeting: "I want to let you know that [person] is no longer with the company. I can't share all the details, but this decision was made after careful consideration. Here's how we're going to handle their responsibilities in the short term. If you have questions or concerns, my door is open."

Don't badmouth the person. Don't share confidential details. But don't leave a vacuum either, because people will fill it with speculation and rumors.

### What Not To Do

### Don't Apologize for Making a Tough Call

"I'm sorry, but I have to let you go."

No. Don't apologize for doing your job. You can express empathy without apologizing for the decision.

"I know this is difficult news" is fine. "I'm sorry I have to do this" makes it sound like you're doing something wrong.

You're not. You're making a necessary business decision.

### Don't Outsource It Unless You Absolutely Have To

If you hired them, you should fire them. Don't make HR or another manager do your difficult work.

I've seen managers who make HR fire people because they don't want to have the conversation. That's not leadership.

If you're the person's manager, you should be the one to deliver the news. It's your responsibility.

The only exception is if there's a safety concern or if the person has threatened violence. In that case, let security or HR handle it.

### Don't Make Promises You Can't Keep

"I'll give you a great reference."

Will you? If you're firing them for performance issues, are you really going to tell their next employer they were great?

Don't make promises in the moment just to make the conversation easier. Be honest about what you can and can't do.

I'll usually say something like, "If someone calls for a reference, I'll confirm your dates of employment and job title. If they ask about performance, I'll be honest about the challenges we discussed."

That's fair. It doesn't leave them hanging, but it doesn't promise something I can't deliver.

### Don't Fire Someone Right Before a Weekend or Holiday

I knew the conventional wisdom is to fire people on Friday so they have the weekend to process. I disagreed.

If you fire someone on Friday, they spend the entire weekend spiraling, unable to take action. They can't start job hunting, they can't talk to HR about questions, they can't do anything productive.

I fire people on Tuesday or Wednesday. It gives them time to process, ask questions, and start taking action before the weekend.

And never, ever fire someone right before a major holiday. That's just cruel.

### The Hardest Firings

Some firings are straightforward. The person was clearly not working out, everyone knew it, and the firing is almost a relief.

But some firings are brutal:

### Firing Someone You Like

I've had to fire people I genuinely liked as humans but who couldn't do the job. These are the hardest because you want to help them, but you can't sacrifice your team or mission for one person.

The key is to separate the personal from the professional. You can like someone and still fire them. In fact, if you like them, you owe them the honesty of telling them this isn't working rather than stringing them along.

**Layoffs**

Firing someone for performance is hard. Firing someone because of budget cuts or restructuring when they've done nothing wrong is worse.

I've done layoffs twice in my career. Both times, I was letting go of people who were doing good work but whose positions were being eliminated. There's no way to make it not difficult.

What I learned: Be honest about why it's happening. Don't hide behind corporate speak. "The organization is restructuring and your position is being eliminated" is better than "We're going in a different direction." And if there's severance, be generous if you can. These people did nothing wrong.

**After the Conversation**

Once you've fired someone, you have about thirty minutes before the rest of your team knows something happened. Use that time wisely.

First, make sure the person's access is handled. This isn't about being cruel — it's about protecting your systems and your team. I've seen fired employees delete files, send inappropriate emails, or worse. Most won't, but you can't take the risk.

Second, prepare yourself for the team conversation. Because that's coming, and how you handle it will determine whether your team trusts you or starts updating their resumes.

---

9

# After the Exit

---

The firing is done. The person is gone. And now you're standing in front of your team, and they're all looking at you with concern and questions.

This is where most managers make mistakes.

They either say too much (violating the fired person's privacy and making everyone uncomfortable) or too little (leaving a vacuum that gets filled with gossip and paranoia). Neither works.

What does work: being direct without oversharing.

**Telling the Team: What to Say**

I gathered the team as soon as possible after the firing — same day if I can, definitely within 24 hours. Waiting longer just lets rumors spread.

I kept it short and factual:

"I want to let you know that [Name] is no longer with the company. Their last day was today. I can't share details about personnel decisions, but I want you to know this was not a decision I made lightly. If you have questions about how this affects your work or the team, I'm happy to discuss that."

That's it. No drama. No details. No "We wish them well in their future endeavors" corporate language that rings hollow.

## What Not to Say

Don't criticize the person. Even if they were difficult, even if everyone knows they were difficult, don't do it. It makes you look petty and makes everyone else wonder what you'll say about them when they're gone.

Don't lie. If someone was fired for performance, don't say they "decided to pursue other opportunities." Your team isn't naive. They know what happened, and lying destroys your credibility.

Don't overshare. "They weren't meeting expectations" is enough. You don't need to detail every mistake they made or every conversation you had with them.

Early in my management career, I made this mistake. I fired someone who had been actively undermining me with the team, and I was so frustrated that I said too much in the team meeting. I didn't criticize them exactly, but I definitely implied they'd been difficult to work with.

One of my best people came to my office afterward and said, "I get that you're frustrated, but that made me uncomfortable. If I ever leave, I don't want to wonder what you'll say about me."

She was right. I apologized to the team the next day. Lesson learned.

## Managing the Emotional Fallout

Even when a firing is justified — even when everyone knew it was coming — it still shakes people up.

Firings remind people that their jobs aren't guaranteed. That they could be next. That you, their friendly manager, are capable of ending someone's livelihood.

Some people will be relieved (especially if the fired person was dragging the team down). Some will be anxious. Some will be upset, especially if they were friends with the person who got fired.

Your job is not to make everyone feel better. Your job is to acknowledge the reality and keep the team moving forward.

I usually did one-on-ones with key team members in the days after a firing. Not to gossip or explain myself, but to check in:

"I know this week has been tough. How are you doing?"

Most people just need to be heard. They need to know you're

aware that this affected them and that you're not just moving on like nothing happened.

### The Gossip Problem

After you fire someone, people will talk.

They'll speculate about why it happened. They'll share their theories. They'll text the fired person to get their side of the story. And some of them will decide you're unfair or that you fire people without good reason.

You can't stop this. But you can contain it.

The key is to be present and available. If you disappear after a firing, people assume you're hiding something. If you're around, business as usual, it signals that this was a necessary decision and life goes on.

I also addressed gossip directly if it gets out of hand. In one situation, a team member was fired for a serious performance issue, and one of their friends on the team was telling everyone that the firing was unfair and politically motivated.

I pulled that person aside and said, "I know you're upset about [Name] leaving. I can't discuss the details with you, but I need you to trust that I don't make these decisions lightly. If you can't do that, we need to talk about whether this is still the right place for you."

It was a hard conversation, but it stopped the gossip immediately.

### Redistributing the Work

When someone leaves, their work doesn't disappear. And your remaining team members are watching to see if you're going to dump it all on them without acknowledgment or support.

I've seen managers handle this poorly. They just quietly reassign the fired person's projects and expect everyone to absorb the extra work with no discussion. That's how you lose your best people.

What I do instead:

First, I make a list of everything the person was working on. Then I figure out what's actually critical and what can wait or be eliminated entirely.

Then I talk to the team: "Here's what [Name] was working on. Here's what needs to be covered immediately, and here's what can wait. I need your help figuring out how to handle this until we hire someone new. I'm not expecting anyone to do two jobs, but I need to know what's realistic."

This does two things: It shows you respect their time, and it gives them agency in the solution.

Sometimes people will volunteer to take on certain projects because they're interested in them. Sometimes you'll realize that half of what the fired person was doing wasn't actually necessary. And sometimes you'll need to bring in temporary help or push back deadlines.

But whatever you do, don't just pile work on people and hope they'll figure it out.

A team member came to me once after a firing and said, "I'm already at capacity. If you need me to take on [Fired Person's] projects, something else has to come off my plate."

She was right. We reprioritized, and I took one of her projects myself. She stayed with the company for three more years and became one of my best hires ever.

**When to Start Looking for a Replacement**

This depends on why you fired the person.

If you fired them because the role wasn't working or you're restructuring, you might not need a replacement at all. Take the time to figure out what you actually need before you start hiring again.

If you fired them because they couldn't do the job, start looking immediately. You need someone in that role, and the longer you wait, the more your team suffers.

But don't rush it. I've seen managers panic-hire after a firing because they're desperate to fill the gap, and they end up with another poor hire. That's worse than leaving the role open.

Take the time to get it right. Your team will respect you more for being thoughtful than for being fast.

**What If You Regret the Decision?**

This is rare, but it happens.

Sometimes you fire someone and then realize you made a

mistake. Maybe you acted too quickly. Maybe you didn't give them enough support. Maybe you were wrong about the situation.

If this happens, you have two options:

1. Admit the mistake and try to bring them back (if they're willing and it makes sense).

2. Accept that it's done and learn from it.

**The Team Is Watching**

Firing someone isn't just about the person you fired. It's about everyone who's left.

They're watching to see how you handle it. They're watching to see if you're fair, if you're honest, if you're capable of making hard decisions without being cruel.

If you handle it well — if you're transparent without oversharing, if you support the team through the transition, if you take responsibility for the decision — you'll earn their respect.

If you handle it poorly — if you disappear, if you dump work on them without acknowledgment, if you speak negatively about the person who left — you'll lose their trust.

Firing someone is hard. The aftermath is harder. But if you do it right, your team will come out stronger on the other side.

---

10

---

# Leadership Sanity Checks

Let's talk about you for a minute.

Because sometimes the problem isn't your team. It's you.

I've seen managers blame their teams for problems they created. I've been that manager. And if you're not willing to look in the mirror and ask yourself hard questions, you're going to keep making the same mistakes.

This chapter is a gut check. If you're honest with yourself, it'll save you from a lot of pain.

**Are You Actually Leading, or Just Managing?**

There's a difference between managing and leading, and most people don't know which one they're doing.

Managing is about processes, tasks, and keeping things running. Leading is about direction, decisions, and taking responsibility when things go wrong.

You need both, but if you're only managing, you're not doing your job.

The test: If you disappeared for a week, would your team know what to do? Would they have a clear sense of priorities and direction, or would they just be waiting for you to tell them what to do next?

If it's the latter, you're micromanaging, not leading.

I learned this when I took over a team that had been micromanaged into oblivion. Every decision, no matter how small, had to go through the previous manager. The team was competent, but they'd been trained not to think for themselves.

It took me six months to undo that damage. I had to actively push decisions back to them, even when it was faster for me to just make the call myself. "What do you think we should do?" became my most-used phrase.

Eventually, they started making decisions without me. And the team got better.

### Are You Giving Feedback, or Just Complaining?

I've worked with managers who constantly complained about their teams but never actually gave them feedback.

"Why can't they just figure this out?" "Why do I have to tell them everything?" "Why don't they take initiative?"

Because you haven't told them what you expect, that's why.

If you're frustrated with someone's performance, ask yourself: Have I actually told them what I need them to do differently? Have I been specific? Have I given them a chance to improve?

If the answer is no, the problem is you.

Feedback isn't a performance review once a year. It's not a vague "You need to be more proactive." It's specific, timely, and actionable.

"When you sent that email to the client without looping me in, it created confusion. Going forward, I need you to cc me on client communications until we're aligned on messaging."

That's feedback. "You need to communicate better" is complaining.

### Are You Playing Favorites?

Everyone has people they like more than others. That's human. But if you're letting that affect how you manage, you're creating problems.

A manager I worked with had a clear favorite on the team. She got the best projects, the most face time with leadership, and endless second chances when she made mistakes. Everyone else got the routine work and harsh feedback for minor issues.

The team hated it. And within a year, half of them had left.

The test: If you wrote down how much time you spend with each team member, how much feedback you give them, and how many opportunities you give them, would it be roughly equal? Or would one or two people get significantly more of your attention?

If it's the latter, you're playing favorites. And your team knows it.

## Are You Protecting Your Team, or Throwing Them Under the Bus?

When something goes wrong, what do you do?

Do you take responsibility and shield your team from the fallout? Or do you point fingers and make sure everyone knows it wasn't your fault?

I've seen managers throw their teams under the bus to save their own reputation. It's damaging, and it destroys trust faster than anything else.

The rule: When your team succeeds, give them the credit. When your team fails, take the blame.

Even if it wasn't your fault. Even if someone on your team made a mistake. You're the leader. It's your responsibility.

A project went sideways once because one of my team members missed a critical deadline. My boss was frustrated and wanted to know who was responsible.

I told him it was on me. I should have been monitoring the timeline more closely. I should have caught the issue earlier.

Was that technically true? Not really. But I wasn't going to throw my team member under the bus. I dealt with the performance issue privately, and I took the heat publicly.

That's what leaders do.

## Are You Hiring People You Can Actually Manage?

Some managers hire people who are smarter or more experienced than them and then feel threatened. They micromanage, undermine, or push those people out.

If you're doing this, you're sabotaging yourself.

Your job is not to be the smartest person in the room. Your job is to build a team that's better than you and then get out of their way.

I hired someone once who had more experience than me in a

critical area. I was nervous about it — what if she made me look bad? What if she didn't respect me?

But I hired her anyway, and she was one of the best decisions I ever made. She made me better. She challenged my thinking. She took projects off my plate that I wasn't good at.

And yes, sometimes she made me look bad. But that's ego talking. The team got better, and that's what mattered.

If you're only hiring people you feel comfortable managing, you're hiring the wrong people.

### Are You Burning Out?

Nobody asks this: Are you okay?

Because if you're not, your team isn't either.

I've seen managers run themselves into the ground trying to do everything themselves. They don't delegate. They don't take time off. They respond to emails at midnight and come in on weekends.

And then they wonder why their team is burned out and disengaged.

You set the tone. If you're working unsustainable hours, your team will feel like they have to as well. If you never take a break, they won't either.

I burned out once. I was working 70-hour weeks, trying to prove I could handle everything. I thought I was being a good leader by being available 24/7.

I wasn't. I was irritable, unfocused, and making bad decisions. And my team was struggling because I was struggling.

It took a very direct conversation with my boss to snap me out of it. He told me I was setting a poor example and that if I didn't take a vacation, he was going to require me to.

I took the vacation. And when I came back, I set boundaries. I stopped responding to emails after 7 PM. I took weekends off. I delegated more.

And my team got better.

### The Hardest Question

One question will tell you everything you need to know about your leadership:

If your team could leave tomorrow with no consequences, how many of them would stay?

Be honest. Not "I think they like working here." Not "They seem happy." If they had a standing offer somewhere else, would they stay because of you, or would they run?

If the answer makes you uncomfortable, it's time to change something.

You can't control everything. You can't make everyone happy. But you can be the kind of leader people want to work for.

And if you're not, that's on you to fix.

# 11

# Building a System That Works

You can't hire and fire your way to a great team. You need a system.

Most managers don't have one. They hire when they're desperate, fire when they're frustrated, and wonder why they keep ending up with the same problems.

A system doesn't mean bureaucracy. It doesn't mean endless processes and forms. It means having a repeatable way to find, evaluate, and develop people that actually works.

**Step 1: Know What You Actually Need**

Before you hire anyone, you need to know what you're hiring for. And I don't mean a job description full of buzzwords. I mean a clear, specific understanding of what this person needs to do and why.

Most job descriptions aren't helpful. They're a laundry list of skills and qualifications that don't tell you anything about what the person will actually be doing.

What I do instead: I write down the three most important things this person needs to accomplish in their first six months. Not skills. Not qualifications. Outcomes.

For example:

• "Build a repeatable process for onboarding new clients that reduces onboarding time by 30%."

• "Take over the monthly reporting so I can focus on strategy."

• "Manage the relationship with our top three clients and ensure renewals."

Once I know what I need them to do, I can figure out what skills and experience they need to do it. But I start with the outcome, not the resume.

## Step 2: Build a Hiring Process You Can Repeat

Most hiring processes are inconsistent. You ask different questions to different candidates. You evaluate people based on gut feel. You make decisions based on who you liked, not who can actually do the job.

That's how you end up with bad hires.

My process:

**1. Phone screen (30 minutes):** I ask the same five questions to every candidate. I'm looking for red flags and basic fit. If they pass, they move on.

**2. Working interview (1-2 hours):** I give them a real problem to solve. Not a case study. Not a hypothetical. A real problem we're facing. I want to see how they think, how they ask questions, and how they handle ambiguity.

**3. Team interview (1 hour):** They meet with 2-3 people they'd be working with. I'm not looking for everyone to love them. I'm looking for whether they can work with the team and whether the team respects them.

**4. Reference checks:** I actually call references. And I ask specific questions, not "Was this person good to work with?"

This process isn't perfect, but it's consistent. And consistency means I can learn from my mistakes and improve over time.

## Step 3: Onboard Like You Mean It

Most onboarding isn't effective because it's not designed to set people up for success. It's designed to check boxes.

What actually matters in the first 30 days:

• **Clarity:** Do they know what they're supposed to be doing? Do they know what success looks like?

- **Support:** Do they have someone they can ask questions without feeling stupid?
- **Quick wins:** Do they have a chance to accomplish something meaningful in the first few weeks?

I give every new hire a 30-day plan. It's not complicated. It's a list of things they need to learn, people they need to meet, and one or two small projects they can complete to build confidence.

And I check in with them every week. Not to micromanage. To make sure they're not drowning.

### Step 4: Give Feedback Early and Often

Most managers wait until something is a big problem before they say anything. By then, it's too late.

I give feedback constantly. Not in a formal, sit-down way. Just in the moment.

"That email was great. I liked how you framed the problem."

"Next time, loop me in before you send something to the client. I want to make sure we're aligned."

"You crushed that presentation. The exec team was impressed."

Feedback doesn't have to be a big deal. It just has to be specific and timely.

And if something is a problem, I address it immediately. Not in three months during a performance review. Immediately.

### Step 5: Know When to Cut Your Losses

Most managers struggle with this: They wait too long to fire people.

They hope the person will improve. They don't want to go through the hiring process again. They feel guilty.

And meanwhile, the rest of the team is suffering.

My rule: If I'm spending more time managing one person than I'm spending on the rest of the team combined, that person needs to go.

It's not about being heartless. It's about being fair to the people who are actually doing their jobs.

### Step 6: Learn from Every Hire (Good and Bad)

Every time I hire someone, I write down why I hired them. What did I see in the interview? What did I think they'd be good at?

Then, six months later, I go back and read it. Was I right? What did I miss? What would I do differently?

This is how you get better at hiring. Not by reading books or taking courses. By paying attention to your own patterns.

I've learned that I'm not great at evaluating charisma. I get charmed by people who interview well, and I overlook red flags because I like them.

So now, when I find myself really liking a candidate, I force myself to slow down. I ask harder questions. I check references more carefully.

That's the system working.

### The System Isn't the Point

Systems aren't magic. They don't guarantee you'll never make a bad hire. They don't make firing people easy.

But they give you a framework. They help you make better decisions more consistently. And they help you learn from your mistakes instead of repeating them.

You don't need a perfect system. You just need one that works for you and that you actually use.

Build it. Refine it. And trust it.

## 12

# The One Thing I Wish I'd Known (And the Stories That Taught Me)

If I could go back and tell my younger self one thing about hiring and firing, it would be this:

**You're going to get it wrong. A lot. And that's okay.**

I spent years thinking that good leaders never made bad hires. That if I just worked harder, asked better questions, and paid more attention, I could avoid mistakes.

I was wrong.

You can do everything right and still hire the wrong person. You can give someone every chance to succeed and still have to fire them. You can be fair, thoughtful, and deliberate, and people will still disagree with your decisions.

That's the job.

And the sooner you accept that, the better you'll be at it.

**The Myth of the Perfect Hire**

Early in my career, I thought hiring was like a puzzle. If I could just find the right combination of skills, experience, and personality, I'd have the perfect team.

So I obsessed over every decision. I interviewed people multiple times. I checked references obsessively. I agonized over every hire like it was a life-or-death decision.

And I still made bad hires.

Take the senior role I needed to fill. The candidate had all the right experience. He'd worked at top companies, had glowing references, and interviewed well. But something felt off. He was polished —too polished. Every answer was perfect. Every story had a neat ending. He never admitted to making a mistake or learning anything the hard way.

I almost passed on him. But I was desperate to fill the role, and on paper, he was exactly what I needed.

So I hired him.

Within three months, I knew I'd made a mistake. He was great at talking about work, but not as effective at actually doing it. He spent more time managing up than managing his team. And when things went wrong, he always had an excuse.

I let him go after six months. It was one of the most expensive mistakes I've made.

Because there's no such thing as a perfect hire. People are complicated. They have good days and bad days. They grow, they change, they surprise you.

The best you can do is make the best decision you can with the information you have, and then deal with the consequences. And trust your gut—if something feels off in the interview, it's probably off. Don't hire someone just because you're desperate.

**The People Who Surprised Me**

But here's what I also learned: Some of my best hires were people I almost didn't hire. They didn't have the right background. They didn't interview perfectly. They didn't check all the boxes.

A woman applied for a leadership role. She'd never managed people before. She was young, didn't have the traditional credentials, and stumbled through parts of the interview.

My boss thought I was making a risky choice. My team was skeptical. Even I wasn't sure.

But something about her stood out. She asked smart questions. She was hungry to learn. And she had a track record of figuring things out when no one showed her how.

I hired her anyway.

She became one of the best leaders I've ever worked with. She built a team from scratch, delivered results ahead of schedule, and earned the respect of people twice her age.

I learned to stop hiring for resumes and start hiring for potential. Don't hire for credentials. Hire for drive, curiosity, resilience—the things you can't see on paper but that make all the difference.

## The Cost of Waiting

The biggest mistake I made early in my career was waiting too long to fire people. I'd see the signs, know it wasn't working, but convince myself one more chance would fix it.

It never did.

One of my team members was brilliant but toxic. He was the best at what he did, but he made everyone around him miserable. He'd undermine people in meetings. He'd refuse to collaborate. He'd complain constantly about how no one else was as good as him.

I knew he was a problem. My team knew he was a problem. But I kept him around because I didn't think I could replace his skills.

Finally, after two of my best people quit because of him, I fired him.

And you know what happened? The team got better. Morale went up. Productivity went up. And we figured out how to do his job without him.

No one is irreplaceable. And keeping a toxic person around because they're good at their job is never worth it.

Meanwhile, my best people had been picking up the slack and losing respect for me. Waiting doesn't help the person struggling— you're just delaying the inevitable. And it definitely doesn't help your team.

If you know it's not working, act. The sooner you do, the less damage it causes.

## The Guilt of Firing

I used to feel terrible every time I fired someone. I'd replay the conversation in my head for days. I'd wonder if I'd given them enough chances, if I'd been too harsh, if I'd negatively impacted their life.

And then one day, a mentor told me something that changed my perspective:

"You're not responsible for their career. You're responsible for your team. And if keeping them around is hurting your team, you're failing the people who are actually doing their jobs."

That didn't make firing people easy. But it made it clear.

I had to fire someone who everyone liked. She was friendly, she showed up on time, and she never caused drama. But she couldn't do the job. She'd been in the role for a year, and despite coaching, feedback, and support, she wasn't improving.

I dreaded the conversation. I thought the team would be upset.

But when I told them, the reaction was... relief. They'd been covering for her for months, and they were exhausted. One person said, "I'm glad you finally did something. We were starting to think you didn't notice."

Your team knows who's not pulling their weight. And if you don't deal with it, they lose respect for you.

Your job is not to save everyone. Your job is to build a team that works. And sometimes that means letting people go.

### The Firing I Regret

But I've also been wrong. I fired an employee who I thought wasn't a culture fit. They were quiet, they didn't socialize with the team, and they seemed disengaged.

Looking back, I was wrong. They weren't disengaged—they were introverted. They did great work, they met every deadline, and they never caused problems.

But I wanted someone who was more "enthusiastic," so I let them go.

A few months later, I realized I'd made a mistake. I'd fired someone for not being like me, not for failing to do their job.

I reached out to apologize and offer a reference. They were gracious about it, but I still feel like I made a poor call.

Don't confuse personality with performance. Just because someone doesn't fit your idea of what a team member should look like doesn't mean they're not doing a good job.

### The Importance of Trusting Yourself

Nobody tells you this about hiring and firing: You're going to get a lot of advice, and most of it won't apply to your situation.

People will tell you to hire for culture fit. Or to hire for skills. Or to never fire someone without a performance improvement plan. Or to fire fast and move on.

And all of that advice might work for someone. But it might not work for you.

You have to figure out what works for your team, your industry, your leadership style. And that means making mistakes, learning from them, and trusting your own judgment.

Early in my career, I hired someone who had more experience than me. He'd been a senior leader at a major company, and I was nervous about managing him.

In our first one-on-one, he said, "I don't need you to tell me how to do my job. I need you to tell me what success looks like and then get out of my way."

It was the best advice I ever got.

I stopped micromanaging. I stopped trying to prove I was smart. I just gave him clear goals and let him figure out how to get there.

He delivered better results than I ever could have, and he made me a better leader in the process.

Your job isn't to be the smartest person on the team. It's to hire people who are smarter than you and then support them.

I used to second-guess every decision. I'd ask for input from everyone, and then I'd get paralyzed trying to make everyone happy.

By the end, I asked for input, I considered it, and then I made the call. And I lived with the consequences.

That's leadership.

**The Hire Who Proved Me Wrong**

I used to think remote work didn't work for certain roles. I thought you needed people in the office to build culture and collaboration.

Then I hired someone who lived across the country. I had no choice—she was the best candidate, and she wasn't willing to relocate.

I was skeptical. But she was more responsive, more productive, and more engaged than half my in-office team.

She proved me wrong. And it made me rethink a lot of my assumptions about how work gets done.

Don't let your preferences get in the way of good hiring. Be willing to challenge your own assumptions.

**What These Stories Taught Me**

Every hire and every firing teaches you something. Sometimes it's a lesson about people. Sometimes it's a lesson about yourself.

The key is to pay attention. Don't just move on to the next hire or the next fire. Take the time to figure out what went right, what went wrong, and what you'd do differently.

That's how you get better.

Earlier, I called out "hire slow, fire fast" in the Foreword—and I meant it. That CEO used it as an excuse to be reckless on both ends. But the advice itself isn't wrong. It's just incomplete without context. So here's what it actually means when you're not using it as a cop-out.

• Hire slower. You'll regret rushing more than you'll regret taking your time—because a bad hire takes far more effort to fix than to prevent. Take the extra time to really understand what the role needs and who's best for it; it saves you from much bigger headaches down the road.

• Fire faster. Waiting doesn't help anyone—the longer you delay, the more damage to morale and productivity. Dragging your feet only prolongs problems and sends a signal to the team that poor performance is tolerated.

• Trust your gut. If something feels off, it probably is. Your instincts sharpen with experience; don't ignore them. As a manager, you'll often have incomplete data—sometimes what you feel is just as important as what you know.

• Don't hire people you can't manage. If you're intimidated by someone, you won't be able to lead them—and your team will sense it. Leadership requires respect both ways; if you can't set expectations or hold someone accountable, it undermines your whole team.

• Don't keep toxic people around just because they're good at their jobs. It's never worth it—the cost to team culture always outweighs the benefit. One toxic high performer can drive away your best people and erode trust faster than you think.

• Give feedback early and often. Don't wait for things to become a crisis; course-correcting early saves everyone pain. People can't improve what they don't know is a problem, and regular feedback helps build trust.

• Take care of your team, but don't sacrifice yourself to save someone who's not willing to do the work. Leadership means knowing when to draw the line. You can support and mentor, but you can't carry someone who isn't committed—it's not fair to you or the rest of the team.

And most importantly: You're going to make mistakes. You're going to make bad hires. You're going to fire people who didn't deserve it. You're going to keep people around too long.

That's okay. Learn from it and move on.

All these lessons, mistakes, and bits of advice add up to something simple.

At the end of the day, hiring and firing isn't about processes or frameworks or perfect decisions.

It's about people. And people are messy.

Your job is to build a team that can do great work together. And sometimes that means making hard decisions that no one will thank you for.

But if you do it with integrity, if you're honest and fair, if you take responsibility when you make mistakes, you'll be okay.

And so will your team.

Now, I've covered the main principles. The framework. The stuff that actually matters when you're building a team and making the calls that keep you up at night. But I know you've still got questions. The ones you don't ask in meetings. The ones you ask yourself at 2 AM or bring up with a trusted friend over a drink. The messy, specific, "what the hell do I do in this exact situation" questions. That's what Chapter 16 is for. No theory. No corporate speak. Just the hard stuff people actually want to know.

## 13

# Bonus Section:
# Answers to Questions
# Nobody Dares to Ask

Let's talk about the questions people ask me in private but never in public. The uncomfortable ones. The ones that don't have clean answers.

Here they are.

**Let's start with the questions that keep you up at night —the ones about your own judgment.**

**"Can I fire someone I just don't like?"**

Here's the truth: you can't fire someone just because you don't like them personally. If they're doing good work, if they're contributing to the team, if the only problem is that you don't enjoy their company—that's not a good reason to fire them.

But if you don't like them because they're toxic, because they undermine you, because they make your team miserable—that's different. That's a performance issue, even if it doesn't look like one on paper.

The question isn't "Do I like this person?" The question is "Is this person making the team better or worse?"

If the answer is worse, you have a reason to act.

**"What if I fire someone and I'm wrong?"**

You might be. I've been wrong before.

But if you've done your due diligence—if you've given feedback, if you've documented the issues, if you've given them a fair chance to improve—then you made the best decision you could with the information you had.

And if you were wrong, you learn from it and do better next time.

Don't let the fear of being wrong paralyze you. Inaction is often worse than making the wrong call.

**"How do I know if I'm being too harsh or too lenient?"**

You probably won't know until you've made a few mistakes in both directions.

If you're too harsh, you'll fire people who could have been great with more support. If you're too lenient, you'll keep people around who are dragging the team down. *The key: pay attention to the outcomes.*

Are you losing good people because they're frustrated with underperformers? That's a sign you're too lenient. Are you burning through hires because no one can meet your standards? That's a sign you're too harsh.

Adjust accordingly.

**Now let's talk about the situations that make this even harder—when personal circumstances get in the way.**

**"What if they're going through something really hard?"**

This is one of the toughest situations you'll face. I've had to fire people who were dealing with sick family members, divorces, financial problems. It's never easy.

But you can't run a team based on people's personal circumstances. If someone can't do the job, they can't do the job.

What you can do is be compassionate about how you do it. Offer severance if you can. Give them time to transition. Provide references if appropriate.

But don't keep someone in a role they can't handle just because you feel bad for them. That's not kindness—it's avoidance, and it's not fair to anyone.

**"How do I fire someone I'm friends with?"**

You probably shouldn't have become friends with them in the

first place. But if you did, and now you have to fire them, here's the reality:

The friendship is probably going to change significantly, if not end entirely.

You can try to preserve it—be honest, compassionate, and clear about why you're making the decision. But don't expect them to understand or forgive you right away.

And don't let the friendship stop you from doing what needs to be done.

### "Should I hire a family member?"

It's almost always a bad idea, even if you think you'll be the exception. Mixing family and business makes honest feedback and fair treatment tricky, and if things go wrong, every family event gets complicated.

But the absolute worst version of this? Hiring an in-law.

Hiring an in-law is the hardest version of hiring family. If things go wrong, you're not just risking your relationship with them— you're risking your relationship with your daughter or sister. They're caught in the middle, and every family gathering can become a minefield. When my colleague finally fired his brother-in-law (after months of missed deadlines), he lost both the working relationship and the family bond. That's what's at stake.

Hiring your own kid or your sibling is complicated. Hiring your son-in-law or brother-in-law is worse.

Here's why: the power dynamic is completely asymmetrical.

If they decide to quit or walk away at the worst possible time, it's just business. Your daughter or sister might be sympathetic to you, but their loyalty is to their spouse. The family relationship stays intact.

But if you need to let them go—because they're underperform- ing, because they've become a problem—now you're not just firing an employee. You're telling your daughter that her husband isn't cutting it. You're putting your sister in a position where she has to choose between supporting you or supporting her spouse.

And here's what makes this uniquely difficult: they know this dynamic exists.

They know that if things go south, you're the one who faces consequences on both sides—professional and personal. They can leave whenever they want. But you can't make the same move without affecting someone you love. That knowledge, even if they never consciously think about it, creates leverage.

When you hire your own family member and it doesn't work out, at least the fallout is contained between you and them. You can have it out, be direct, and eventually move past it.

But when you hire an in-law, you're not just risking your relationship with them. You're risking your relationship with your daughter or your sister—the person you actually love, who is married to this person.

Fire your son-in-law, and your daughter is caught in the middle. She loves you. She loves him. Now she has to navigate the fact that her father thinks her husband isn't working out. Every family dinner becomes a minefield. Every holiday is tense. She feels like she has to choose sides.

A colleague of mine hired his brother-in-law to run operations. The guy was struggling—missed deadlines, couldn't manage the team. But my colleague couldn't bring himself to address it because he knew what it would do to his relationship with his sister.

When he finally did fire him, it was worse than if he'd done it earlier. His sister felt betrayed. The brother-in-law felt humiliated. And my colleague lost both the working relationship and the family relationship.

Now they don't talk. Holidays are divided.

That's what you're risking when you hire an in-law.

If you absolutely must hire an in-law, do three things before they start: put expectations in writing, agree on how performance will be measured, and decide together what happens if it doesn't work out. Spell it all out—otherwise, you're risking more than just the business; every family memory is on the table.

Just know what you're signing up for. It's not just business on the line—it's every birthday, every wedding, every family memory that might get affected.

**Takeaway:** Family and business don't mix—especially with in-laws. If you ignore this, set expectations in stone before the first day.

**Let's shift to the practical fears—the legal and procedural questions that make managers hesitate.**

**"What if I'm scared I'll get sued?"**

This is a real concern, and you should take it seriously.

Document everything. Give clear feedback. Follow your company's policies. Consult with HR or legal before you fire anyone.

But don't let fear of legal action stop you from making necessary decisions. Most wrongful termination lawsuits happen when managers don't document issues or fire people without warning.

If you've done your job—if you've been clear, fair, and consistent—you'll be in a much better position.

**Quick Checklist for Protecting Yourself Legally:**

• Document all performance issues and conversations.

• Give clear, written feedback and improvement plans.

• Follow your company's procedures for warnings and terminations.

• Consult HR or legal before taking action.

• Keep records organized and accessible.

When in doubt, write it down and ask for backup.

**"Is it ever okay to fire someone on the spot?"**

In cases of serious misconduct—such as theft, harassment, violence, or significant ethical violations—yes. You don't need a performance improvement plan for that.

But for performance issues? No. You owe people a chance to improve, and you owe yourself the documentation to protect against legal issues.

**"Does it ever get easier?"**

No. And if it does, you should probably stop managing people.

Firing someone should never feel easy or routine. If you stop caring about the impact it has on people's lives, you've lost something important.

But it does get clearer. You get better at knowing when it's necessary. You get better at handling the conversation. You get better at moving forward afterward.

It doesn't get easier. But you get better at it.

**"What's the worst firing you've ever done?"**

I fired someone two weeks before Christmas once. It was a performance issue that had been building for months, and I'd given them multiple chances to improve.

But the timing was difficult. I knew it. They knew it. And I still think about it.

Could I have waited until January? Maybe. But waiting would have been unfair to the rest of the team, who were covering for this person during the busiest time of the year.

I made the call. It was hard. And I'd probably make the same decision again.

**Now, what about how your team sees you when you make these calls?**

**"What if my team thinks I'm a terrible person for firing someone?"**

They might. Especially if they were friends with the person you fired.

But your job isn't to be liked. It's to make the right decisions for the team.

If you fired someone for good reasons, and you handled it professionally, your team will respect you even if they don't like the decision.

And if they don't, that's something you'll have to live with.

**"Can I rehire someone I fired?"**

Short answer: probably not.

Longer answer: most people who do it regret it. If you fired someone because they weren't ready for the role and they've grown since, it might work. But if the issue was performance or behavior, bringing them back rarely ends well.

**Finally, let's talk about the bigger questions—the ones that make you wonder if this is even the right job for you.**

**"What if I just don't want to deal with this?"**

Then you should reconsider whether management is the right path for you.

I'm not saying this to be harsh. Hiring and firing is part of the job. If you're not willing to do it, you're not doing your job.

And that's okay. Not everyone is cut out for management. There's no shame in stepping back into an individual contributor role if that's a better fit.

But if you're going to lead people, you have to make hard decisions. There's no way around it.

**"What if I'm the one being fired?"**

If you're being fired: don't argue in the moment, don't burn bridges, and process your feelings later. It's a shock, even if you saw it coming—but it doesn't define you. What matters is what you do next: update your résumé, reach out to your network, and be honest (but not bitter) in interviews. "It wasn't the right fit" is enough. Don't badmouth your old boss or company, but don't lie either.

You'll be okay. Sometimes, getting fired is the push you need to find something better. Just don't let this moment define the rest of your career.

**Final Thought**

There are no perfect answers to these questions. Every situation is different. Every person is different.

But if you approach hiring and firing with honesty, fairness, and a willingness to take responsibility for your decisions, you'll be okay.

And so will your team.

# 14

# Further Reading & Resources

I didn't figure this out alone. I made mistakes, read books looking for answers, and stole what worked. Most books I read were forgettable. A few changed how I thought. Some I disagreed with but learned from anyway.

Here's what actually mattered—and why.

**On Hiring**

*Who: The A Method for Hiring* by Geoff Smart and Randy Street (2008)

This book will save you from wasting months on bad hires. If your interview process is a mess—different questions for every candidate, relying on gut feel, wondering why you keep getting it wrong—start here.

Smart and Street give you a framework you can actually use: define the role clearly, source systematically, interview with structure. Their "chronological interview" technique—walking through someone's entire career and asking what they did, how they did it, and who can verify it—forces people to get specific instead of giving rehearsed answers.

Steal their questions. "What were you hired to do? What did you actually accomplish? What were you proud of? What would your boss say about you?" Simple, but it works.

The book assumes you have HR support and recruiting budgets, which you might not have. But even if you only steal the interview framework, it's worth it. This is the one hiring book I recommend without hesitation.

*The Hiring Problem* by Peter Cappelli (2019)

Cappelli tears apart everything broken about modern recruiting —the credential obsession, the endless filters, the assumption that more process means better hires. He's right about almost all of it, and reading it will make you feel less crazy.

If you've been frustrated watching companies reject great candidates because they didn't have the "right" degree or because they'd been out of work for six months, Cappelli will validate what you already suspect: most hiring processes are designed to eliminate risk, not find talent.

The problem is he's better at diagnosis than solutions. You'll finish the book angry at how broken everything is, but without a clear path forward. Still, understanding why your process keeps failing is half the battle. Read this after a particularly bad hiring cycle and use it to see what you need to change.

*Radical Candor* by Kim Scott (2017)

This book will give you language for something you might be doing instinctively but inconsistently: caring about people while still being direct about problems. Scott's framework—care personally, challenge directly—is what I've been saying throughout this entire book.

What you should steal: her approach to feedback. Don't sugarcoat. Don't wait. Don't make it about their personality. Just tell them what's not working and why it matters. Use this every time you have to tell someone their work isn't good enough.

Where I disagreed: Scott assumes you're working in a culture that can handle candor. If you're in a passive-aggressive organization where people smile to your face and undermine you behind your back, trying to implement radical candor will get you labeled as "difficult" or "abrasive." You have to build trust first, and that takes time.

But it will change how you think about feedback. If you soften bad news too much, trying to protect people's feelings, this book will help you realize that clarity is kindness. People deserve to know where they stand.

### On Firing and Hard Conversations

*Crucial Conversations* by Kerry Patterson, Joseph Grenny, Ron McMillan, and Al Switzler (2002)

Read this before your next firing goes badly. If you've ever handled a termination conversation poorly—got defensive, made it personal, left them confused about what actually happened—this book will teach you how to prepare for hard conversations without making things worse.

The framework is solid: get clear on what you want, understand what the other person might be thinking, and stay in dialogue instead of shutting down. Most people avoid hard conversations because they're afraid of conflict. This book teaches you that avoiding the conversation is worse than having it.

The downside: it's dense and academic. You'll have to work through it. But if you're the type who dreads difficult conversations and likely to avoid them, and that's worth something.

### On Leadership

*Good to Great* by Jim Collins (2001)

Read this if you want to understand why some teams pull ahead and others stagnate. Collins studied companies that went from good to great and found patterns: they got the right people on the bus, they faced brutal facts about reality, and they had clarity about what they could be best at.

The hiring and firing implications are huge. You can't build a great team if you're keeping people around out of loyalty or fear of conflict. You can't move forward if you're not honest about who's pulling their weight and who's not.

The culture will change because the behavior changes.

### On Understanding People

*Thinking, Fast and Slow* by Daniel Kahneman (2011)

This book will make you question every hiring decision you've ever made. Kahneman explains cognitive biases—the shortcuts our brains take that often lead us astray. We hire people who remind us of ourselves. We overweight first impressions. We see patterns that aren't there.

If you want to understand why you keep making the same hiring mistakes, or why candidates who look perfect on paper bomb in interviews, or why you believe the stories people give in interviews and reference checks, read this.

## On Systems

*The Goal* by Eliyahu M. Goldratt (1984)

This is a novel about a factory manager trying to figure out why his plant is underperforming even though everyone seems competent. It's about systems thinking—understanding that a team is only as strong as its weakest link, and that optimizing one part often breaks another.

If you've hired good people and given them clear roles but the team still isn't performing, read this. It will help you see the bottlenecks you're missing.

## On Legal Protection

*The Essential HR Handbook* by Sharon Armstrong and Barbara Mitchell (2008)

This is dry, but it matters. Most wrongful termination lawsuits happen because managers didn't document problems or didn't follow their own procedures. This book walks you through what you need to do to protect yourself and your company.

People claim they were never warned about problems. You claim you told them repeatedly. Who wins? The person with documentation.

## A Final Note

These books will probably help you. But they're not a substitute for experience. You'll learn more from your mistakes than from any book. The goal is to make fewer of them, and to come back better. That's what your team will remember.

# Bibliography

Armstrong, S., & Mitchell, B. (2008). *The essential HR handbook*. Career Press.

Cappelli, P. (2019). *The hiring problem*. Wharton Digital Press.

Collins, J. (2001). *Good to great: Why some companies make the leap... and others don't*. Harper-Business.

Coyle, D. (2018). *The culture code: The secrets of highly successful groups*. Bantam.

Goldratt, E. M. (1984). *The goal: A process of ongoing improvement*. North River Press.

Kahneman, D. (2011). *Thinking, fast and slow*. Farrar, Straus and Giroux.

Lencioni, P. (2002). *The five dysfunctions of a team: A leadership fable*. Jossey-Bass.

Patterson, K., Grenny, J., McMillan, R., & Switzler, A. (2002). *Crucial conversations: Tools for talking when stakes are high*. McGraw-Hill.

Scott, K. (2017). *Radical candor: Be a kick-ass boss without losing your humanity*. St. Martin's Press.

Smart, G., & Street, R. (2008). *Who: The A method for hiring*. Ballantine Books.

Stone, D., Patton, B., & Heen, S. (1999). *Difficult conversations: How to discuss what matters most*. Penguin Books.

Voss, C., & Raz, T. (2016). *Never split the difference: Negotiating as if your life depended on it*. Harper Business.